Introduction
Flat Stanley

Story Notes

Flat Stanley: With wit and imagination, author Jeff Brown brings us Stanley—a boy who lives in the flat lane. After waking up one morning to find he's been flattened by a wayward bulletin board, Flat Stanley has many unusual, unbelievable, and flat-out absurd adventures!

We hope your students enjoy this inventive tale.

CAUTION (Reminder)

Do not read the Read Aloud recommendations during small group instruction. Reserve this time for students to read.

Recommended Read Alouds

The *Read Well 2* suggested Read Alouds enhance small group instruction—providing opportunities to further build background knowledge and vocabulary.

Sideways Stories from Wayside School by Louis Sachar
Fiction • Narrative

The Wayside School is a strange school—it was built sideways by mistake, with its 30 classrooms stacked on top of each other. The stories are a bit strange too. Poor Jason is stuck to his seat by a large wad of gum. Kathy assumes that no one will ever like her, and she turns out to be right.

Read Well Connections
Like *Flat Stanley*, the stories in this Read Aloud feature improbable events told in a matter-of-fact voice. Students will enjoy the quirky humor and the fanciful tales.

NOTE FROM THE AUTHORS

THIRD GRADE LEVEL PLUS!

Students at three field test sites who began the year with *Read Well Fluency Foundations* showed impressive gains throughout the school year. Upon completion of Unit 17, these students scored, on average, a 3.7 grade equivalency on the Woodcock Reading Mastery (WRM) Short Scale, Total Reading (Word Identification and Passage Comprehension). Pre- and post-test scores demonstrated an overall gain of 1.6 on grade equivalence.

Field test students who completed *Flat Stanley* rose from the 61st percentile to the 71st percentile on the WRM Total Reading test and jumped from the 54th percentile to the 69th percentile in comprehension scores.

If your students have been taught to criterion, as measured by the Oral Reading Fluency Assessments, there is much to celebrate. It is highly likely that your students are already at or above a third grade equivalence.

New and Important Objectives
A Research-Based Reading Program

Phonemic Awareness

Phonics

Fluency

Vocabulary

Comprehension

Phonological and Phonemic Awareness

Blending; Rhyming; Onset and Rime; Counting Syllables

Phonics

Cumulative Letter Sounds and Combinations

Review • Ss, Ee, ee, Mm, Aa, Dd, th, Nn, Tt, Ww, Ii, Th, Hh, Cc, Rr, ea, sh, Sh, Kk, -ck, oo, ar, wh, Wh, ĕ, -y (as in fly), Ll, Oo, Bb, all, Gg, Ff, Uu, er, oo (as in book), Yy, a (schwa), Pp, ay, Vv, Qq, Jj, Xx, or, Zz, a_e, -y (as in baby), i_e, ou, ow (as in cow), ch, Ch, ai, igh, o_e, ir, aw, ew, ue, u_e, ow (as in snow), ge, -dge, ci, ce, kn, ph, oa, oi, ea (as in bread), gi, au, oy

Cumulative Affixes, Morphographs, and Open Syllables

Review • -ed, -en, -er, -es, -est, -ing, -ly, -s, -y, -tion, re-, un-, ex-, o (as in open), -ful, bi-, de-, -able, i (as in silence), be-, dis-, -ous, -al, -ible, -or, -ment, -ic, pre-, -ity, -sion, -ness, -less

★ New Letter Sounds, Combinations, Affixes, and Morphographs

in- (as in insert) • increase, insert, insurance

im- (as in impossible) • impure

★ New Proper Nouns

Agnes, Christmas, Dr. Dan, Encyclopaedia Britannica, Famous Museum of Art, Harry, Jeffreys, Lambchops, Little Bo Peep, Max, Mr. Dart, Mr. Dart's, Mr. Lambchop, Mr. Lambchop's, Mr. O. Jay Dart, Mrs. Lambchop, Mrs. O. Jay Dart, Penelope, Policemen's Ball, Postal Service, Stanley Lambchop, Stanley's, Thomas Anthony Jeffrey

★ New Pattern Words

◆ bars, beard, bearded ◆ blush, board ◆ cheaper ◆ cheeks, clamp, clamped, creak, creaking, crept, curve ◆ drunk, eh, flakes, flung, fork, frame, gang ◆ glow, goof, goop ◆ gosh, grate, grating, haste, hay ◆ jail, joke, kite, kites, loop, nurse, phases, pitch, poof, rap, rapped, ripped, sash ◆ shaft, slot, sneak, soaked, speed, speeding, spool ◆ sport, stamps, strode, trudge, trudged, whilst, wits'

*Known Pattern Words With Affixes • banged, blowing, bounded, bulged, causes, cries, crowds, curls, dislike, edges, faced, guards, gusts, hopeless, hoping, hurting, hurts, laces, larger, lightly, loudest, matched, mixed, moaned, piled, popping, pumped, pumping, rounded, ruder, rules, sharply, shooting, shorter, showing, sliding, smiling, strongly, swooped, tiring, toasts, toys, training, tunes, undid, unrolled, unrolling, whooshing, woken

---

* **Known Pattern Words With Affixes, Known Tricky Words With Affixes,** and **Known Multisyllabic Words With Affixes** have base words students have previously read. The words are new in this unit because they have not been previously read with the affix.

★ = New in this unit

◆ = Words that are not introduced in the exercises before they are read in the storybook

READ WELL®

Flat Stanley

Teacher's Guide

Unit 19

in- • as in <u>in</u>sert	im- • Means not, as in <u>im</u>possible

Note: See New and Important Objectives on page 2 for a complete list of skills taught and reviewed.

Critical Foundations in Primary Reading

Marilyn Sprick, Ann Watanabe, Karen Akiyama-Paik, and Shelley V. Jones

Sopris West®
EDUCATIONAL SERVICES

A Cambium Learning® Company

BOSTON, MA · LONGMONT, CO

ISBN 13-digit: 978-1-60218-542-5
ISBN 10-digit: 1-60218-542-5

6 7 8 9 RRDHRBVA 14 13 12 11 10

167020/1-10

Table of Contents
Unit 19
Flat Stanley

Letter Sounds and Combinations

Cumulative Review of *Read Well 1* Sounds and Combinations (Ss, Ee, ee, Mm, Aa, Dd, th, Nn, Tt, Ww, Ii, Th, Hh, Cc, Rr, ea, sh, Sh, Kk, -ck, oo, ar, wh, Wh, ĕ, -y as in fly, Ll, Oo, Bb, all, Gg, Ff, Uu, er, oo as in book, Yy, a schwa, Pp, ay, Vv, Qq, Jj, Xx, or, Zz, a_e, -y as in baby, i_e, ou, ow as in cow, ch, Ch, ai, igh, o_e, ir) and:

Unit 2	Unit 3		Unit 5	Unit 6
aw /aw/ **Paw** Voiced	**ew** /ōō/ **Crew** Voiced	**ue** /ōō/ **Blue** Voiced	**u_e** /ōō/ **Flute** Bossy E Voiced	**ow** /ōōō/ **Snow** Voiced (Long)	**ge** /j/ **Page** Voiced

Unit 6	Unit 7		Unit 8		Unit 10
-dge /j/ **Badge** Voiced	**ci** /sss/ **Circle** Unvoiced	**ce** /sss/ **Center** Unvoiced	**kn** /nnn/ **Knee** Voiced	**ph** /fff/ **Phone** Unvoiced	**oa** /ōōō/ **Boat** Voiced (Long)

Unit 11		Unit 12		Unit 13
oi /oi/ **Point** Voiced	**ea** /ĕĕĕ/ **Bread** Voiced (Short)	**gi** /j/ **Giraffe** Voiced	**au** /au/ **Astronaut** Voiced	**oy** /oy/ **Boy** Voiced

Affixes (including morphographs—affixes taught with meaning) and Open Syllables

Cumulative Review of *Read Well 1* Affixes (-ed, -en, -es, -ing, -ly, -s, -y, -tion) and:

Unit 2	Unit 3		Unit 5		Unit 6
re- **Means again** as in reread	**un-** **Means not** as in unhappy	**ex-** as in excited	**o** Open syllable /ō/ as in open and moment	**-ful** **Means full of** as in colorful	**bi-** **Means two** as in bicycle

Unit 7	Unit 8	Unit 11	Unit 12	Unit 13	
de- as in detective	**-able** as in comfortable	**i** Open syllable /ī/ as in silence and pilot	**be-** as in before	**-ous** as in enormous	**dis-** as in discover

Unit 14		Unit 15		Unit 16	
-al as in animal	**-ible** as in flexible	**-or** **Means one who** as in actor	**-ment** as in apartment	**-ic** as in scientific	**pre-** **Means before** as in preview

Unit 17		Unit 18		Unit 19	
-ity as in activity	**-sion** as in permission	**-ness** as in fairness	**-less** **Means without** as in helpless	**in-** as in insert	**im-** **Means not** as in impossible

Phonics (continued)

★ New Compound and Hyphenated Words

afternoons ◆ airmail ◆ bookcase ◆ downtown ◆ football, half-horse, half-man, handcuffed, meanwhile, moonlight, nobody ◆ overheated ◆ pancake, pitch-dark, policeman, policemen, rainbow ◆ roller-skating, round-trip, sideways, snowboard, someplace ◆ toothbrush, trapdoor ◆ understood ◆ wallpaper, yo-yo

★ Other New Multisyllabic Words

absurd, alter, altered, anger, angrily, apologize, apologized, arrested, bandanna, beneath, bulletin, capture, civilized ◆ closet, college, control, darndest, decorate, direct, disgust, disgusted, emotion, envelope, examination, experience ◆ favor ◆ feller, flashy, floppy, fragile, furious, further, gloomy, handle, handled, hasty, heaven, jostle ◆ lantern, limber, lower, lowered, manage, managed, markings, marvel, medal, messages ◆ opposite, pajama, parcel, phooey, pizzazz, pleasant, polite, politeness, prickle, prickly, recently, religion, remarks, ringlets, saucers, sensational, shepherdess, shepherdesses, sneakery, sneaky ◆ soda, suspect, tailor, ticket, tickets, trousers, velvet, violin, volume, volumes

*Known Multisyllabic Words With Affixes • accidentally, balancing, cleverly, directors, doctors, enjoyable, enjoyed, gracefully, hurrying, lettered, models, noticing, ordinarily, presents, quieter, quivery, respects, robbers, subjects, tangling, taxis, tickly, tireder, unexpected, windy

★ New Tricky Words

borrowed, cuckoo, fierce, furious, jealous, measurements, mirror, ought, pleasure, roughly, straightened, terrifying

*Known Tricky Words With Affixes • believable, brother's, climbed, eights, proved, terribly, unbelievable, wearing, younger

Fluency

Accuracy, Expression, Phrasing, Rate

Vocabulary

New • absurd, accidentally, alter, civilized, cleverness, disgusted, entrance, fierce, fragile, furious, gloomy, hasty, jealous, jostle, limber, manage, marvel, occasion, ordinarily, ought, parcel, patient, perhaps, pleasant, polite, politeness, recently, recognize, reply, round-trip, rudeness, rummage, sensational, strode, suspect, volume

Review • adventure, amazing, approximately, Australia, brag, definitely, despite, disguise, distressed, embarrassed, examine, fascinating, impressed, ordinary, permission, popular, speechless, unique, valuable

Reviewed in Context • absolutely, adventure, allow, amazed, amazing, bird's-eye view, chain of events, commotion, community, dangerous, dawdle, despite, dinosaur, disguise, examine, except, flexible, Ghana, impossible, impressed, manners, obey, panic, perfect, permission, pretend, realize, respect, tall tale, unique, valuable, wonderful

Idioms and Expressions

New • enough is enough

Comprehension

Unit Genres
Fiction • Imaginative

Comprehension Processes
Build Knowledge: Factual, Procedural, Conceptual

Day	1	2	3	4	5	6	7
Remember							
Defining							
Identifying (recalling)	S,C	S,C	S,C	S,C	S,C	S,C	C
Using							
Understand							
Defining (in your own words)	S	S	S,C	S			
Describing	S,C		S	S			
Explaining (rephrasing)	S	S	S	S,C	S,C	S	S
Illustrating							
Sequencing					C		C
Summarizing		S,C	S		S	S	C
Using	S,C	S	S,C	S	S,C	S,C	C
Visualizing	S						
Apply							
Demonstrating				S	S		
Explaining (unstated)	S	S	S	S,C	C	S	
Illustrating	C			C			
Inferring	S	S	S	S,C		S	C
Making Connections (relating)	S		S	S	S		
Predicting	S	S	S	S	S	S	
Using	S	S,C	S	S,C	S	S	
Analyze							
Classifying							
Comparing/Contrasting	S						
Distinguishing Cause/Effect	C	S					
Drawing Conclusions		S	S				
Inferring							
Evaluate							
Making Judgments							
Responding (personal)		C	C	C	C	S,C	
Create							
Generating Ideas	C	C	S,C	C		S,C	

E = Exercise, S = Storybook, C = Comprehension & Skill

Comprehension (continued)

Skills and Strategies

Day	1	2	3	4	5	6	7
Priming Background Knowledge							
Setting a Purpose for Reading		S	S	S	S	S	
Answering Questions	S,C	S	S	S	S	S	
Asking Questions						C	
Visualizing							
Comprehension Monitoring/Fix Ups							
Does it Make Sense?	C	C	C	C	C		
Looking Back							
Restating							
Summarizing							
Main Idea							
Retelling							
Supporting Details		C					
Understanding Text Structure							
Title, Author, Illustrator	S,C	S	S			S	
Fact or Fiction							
Genre (Classifying)							
Narrative							
Setting					C		
Main Character/Traits (Characterization)	S,C	C		C			
Goal							
Problem/Solution		S		S	S	S	
Action/Events/Sequence	S		S	C	S,C	S	C
Outcome/Conclusion					S	S	
Lesson/Author's Message							S,C
Expository							
Subject/Topic							
Heading							
Supporting Details (Facts/Information)		C					
Main Idea							
Using Graphic Organizers							
Chart							
Diagram (labeling)							
Hierarchy (topic/detail)		C					
K-W-L							
Map (locating, labeling)							
Matrix (compare/contrast)							
Sequence (linear, cycle, cause and effect)	C				C		C
Story Map							
Web	C						

E = Exercise, S = Storybook, C = Comprehension & Skill

Comprehension (continued)

Study Skills

Day	1	2	3	4	5	6	7
Alphabetical Order							
Following Directions							
Locating Information	C		S				
Note Taking							
Previewing							
Reviewing		S	S	S	S	S	
Test Taking		C					C
Using Glossary							
Using Table of Contents	S						
Viewing	S	S	S	S			
Verifying							

Writing in Response to Reading

Day	1	2	3	4	5	6	7
Sentence Completion	C	C	C	C	C	C	C
Making Lists							
Sentence Writing				C	C	C	C
Story Retell/Summary						C	C
Fact Summary							
Paragraph Writing					C		C
Report Writing							
Open-Ended Response		C	C	C	C	C	
Creative Writing		C	C	C			

Writing Traits

(Addressed within the context of Writing in Response to Reading)

Day	1	2	3	4	5	6	7
Ideas and Content							
Elaborating/Generating	C	C	C	C	C	C	
Organization							
Introduction							
Topic Sentence							
Supporting Details							
Sequencing					C		
Word Choice							
Sophisticated Words (Tier 2 and 3)	C	C	C	C		C	
Conventions							
Capital	C	C	C	C	C	C	C
Ending Punctuation	C	C	C	C	C	C	C
Other (commas, quotation marks)							
Presentation							
Handwriting	C	C	C	C	C	C	C
Neatness	C	C	C	C	C	C	C

E = Exercise, S = Storybook, C = Comprehension & Skill

Daily Lesson Planning

LESSON PLAN FORMAT

Teacher-Directed 45 Minutes		Independent Teacher-Directed, as needed
Lesson Part 1 (Phonological Awareness, Phonics, Fluency, Comprehension) 15–20 Minutes	**Lesson Part 2** (Vocabulary, Fluency, Comprehension) 20–25 Minutes	**Lesson Part 3** (Vocabulary, Fluency, Comprehension) 15–20 Minutes
• Exercises	• Unit and/or Story Opener • Vocabulary • Interactive Story Reading • Short Passage Practice Timed Readings	• Story Reading With Partner or Whisper Reading • Comprehension and Skill Activities

HOMEWORK

Read Well Homework (blackline masters of new *Read Well 2* passages) provides an opportunity for children to celebrate accomplishments with parents. Homework should be sent home on routine days.

ORAL READING FLUENCY ASSESSMENT

Upon completion of this unit, assess each student and proceed to Unit 20, as appropriate.

WRITTEN ASSESSMENT

During the time students would normally complete Comprehension and Skill Activities, students will be administered a Written Assessment that can be found on page 123 in the students' *Activity Book 3*.

Note: See Making Decisions for additional assessment information.

DIFFERENTIATED LESSON PLANS

The differentiated lesson plans illustrate how to use materials for students with various learning needs. As you set up your unit plan, always include *Read Well 2* Exercises and Story Reading on a daily basis. Unit 19 includes 7-, 9-, 10-, and 11-Day Plans.

Plans	For groups that:
7-DAY	Complete Oral Reading Fluency Assessments with Passes and Strong Passes
9-DAY	Complete Oral Reading Fluency Assessments with Passes and require teacher-guided assistance with Story Reading and Comprehension and Skill Work
10-, 11-, or 12-DAY	Have difficulty passing the unit Oral Reading Fluency Assessments

7-DAY PLAN

Day 1

Teacher-Directed
- Exercise 1
- Story Opener: Flat Stanley
- Vocabulary, Ch. 1
- Flat Stanley, Ch. 1
- Guide practice, as needed, on Book Journal Cover, Entry 1, Comp & Skill 1

Independent Work
- Repeated Reading, Partner or Whisper Read, Flat Stanley, Ch. 1
- Book Journal Entry 1, Comp & Skill 1

Homework
- Homework Passage 1

Day 2

Teacher-Directed
- Exercise 2
- Vocabulary, Ch. 2
- Flat Stanley, Ch. 2, pages 8–15
- Guide practice, as needed, on Book Journal Entry 2, Comp & Skill 2

Independent Work
- On Your Own: Partner or Whisper Read, Flat Stanley, Ch. 2, pages 16–21
- Book Journal Entry 2, Comp & Skill 2

Homework
- Homework Passage 2

Day 3

Teacher-Directed
- Exercise 3
- Vocabulary, Ch. 3
- Flat Stanley, Ch. 3, pages 22–27
- Guide practice, as needed, on Book Journal Entry 3, Comp & Skill 3

Independent Work
- On Your Own: Partner or Whisper Read, Flat Stanley, Ch. 3, pages 28–33
- Book Journal Entry 3, Comp & Skill 3

Homework
- Homework Passage 3

Day 4

Teacher-Directed
- Exercise 4
- Vocabulary, Ch. 4, pages 34–45
- Flat Stanley, Ch. 4, pages 34–39
- Guide practice, as needed, on Book Journal Entry 4, Comp & Skill 4

Independent Work
- On Your Own: Partner or Whisper Read, Flat Stanley, Ch. 4, pages 39–45
- Book Journal Entry 4, Comp & Skill 4

Homework
- Homework Passage 4

Day 5

Teacher-Directed
- Exercise 5
- Vocabulary, Ch. 4, pages 46–53
- Flat Stanley, Ch. 4, pages 46–49
- Guide practice, as needed, on Book Journal Entry 5, Comp & Skill 5

Independent Work
- On Your Own: Partner or Whisper Read, Flat Stanley, Ch. 4, pages 49–53
- Book Journal Entry 5, Comp & Skill 5

Homework
- Homework Passage 5

Day 6

Teacher-Directed
- Exercise 6
- Vocabulary, Ch. 5
- Flat Stanley, Ch. 5, pages 54–60
- Guide practice, as needed, on Book Journal Entry 6, Comp & Skill 6

Independent Work
- On Your Own: Partner or Whisper Read, Flat Stanley, Ch. 5, pages 60–65
- Book Journal Entry 6, Comp & Skill 6

Homework
- Homework Passage 6

Day 7

Teacher-Directed
- Exercise 7
- Fluency, Prickly Penelope (Exercise 7b)

Independent Work
- Repeated Reading: Partner or Whisper Read, Fluency, Prickly Penelope (Exercise 7b)
- Written Assessment
- Oral Reading Fluency Assessment*

Homework
- Homework Passage 7

* The Oral Reading Fluency Assessments are individually administered by the teacher while students are working on their Written Assessments.

9-DAY PLAN • *Pre-Intervention*

Day 1

Teacher-Directed
- Exercise 1
- Story Opener: Flat Stanley
- Vocabulary, Ch. 1
- Flat Stanley, Ch. 1
- Guide practice on Book Journal Cover, Entry 1, Comp & Skill 1

Independent Work
- Repeated Reading, Partner or Whisper Read, Flat Stanley, Ch. 1
- Book Journal Entry 1, Comp & Skill 1

Homework
- Homework Pass. 1

Day 2

Teacher-Directed
- Exercise 2
- Vocabulary, Ch. 2
- Flat Stanley, Ch. 2, pages 8–15
- Guide practice on Book Journal Entry 2, Comp & Skill 2

Independent Work
- On Your Own: Partner or Whisper Read, Flat Stanley, Ch. 2, pages 16–21
- Book Journal Entry 2, Comp & Skill 2

Homework
- Homework Passage 2

Day 3

Teacher-Directed
- Exercise 3
- Vocabulary, Ch. 3
- Flat Stanley, Ch. 3, pages 22–27
- Guide practice on Comp & Skill 3

Independent Work
- Repeated Reading: Partner or Whisper Read, Flat Stanley, Ch. 3, pages 22–27
- Comp & Skill 3

Homework
- Extra Practice Word Fluency A

Day 4

Teacher-Directed
- Review Exercise 3
- Vocabulary, Ch. 3
- Flat Stanley, Ch. 3, pages 28–33
- Guide practice on Book Journal Entry 3

Independent Work
- Repeated Reading: Partner or Whisper Read, Flat Stanley, Ch. 3, pages 28–33
- Book Journal Entry 3

Homework
- Homework Passage 3

Day 5

Teacher-Directed
- Exercise 4
- Vocabulary, Ch. 4, pages 34–35
- Flat Stanley, Ch. 4, pages 34–39
- Guide practice on Book Journal Entry 4, Comp & Skill 4

Independent Work
- On Your Own: Partner or Whisper Read, Flat Stanley, Ch. 4, pages 39–45
- Book Journal Entry 4, Comp & Skill 4

Homework
- Homework Pass. 4

Day 6

Teacher-Directed
- Exercise 5
- Vocabulary, Ch. 4, pages 46–53
- Flat Stanley, Ch. 4, pages 46–49
- Guide practice on Book Journal Entry 5, Comp & Skill 5

Independent Work
- On Your Own: Partner or Whisper Read, Flat Stanley, Ch. 4, pages 49–53
- Book Journal Entry 5, Comp & Skill 5

Homework
- Homework Pass. 5

Day 7

Teacher-Directed
- Exercise 6
- Vocabulary, Ch. 5
- Flat Stanley, Ch. 5, pages 54–60
- Guide practice on Comp & Skill 6

Independent Work
- Repeated Reading: Partner or Whisper Read, Flat Stanley, Ch. 5, pages 54–60
- Comp & Skill 6

Homework
- Extra Practice Word Fluency B

Day 8

Teacher-Directed
- Review Exercise 6
- Vocabulary, Ch. 5
- Flat Stanley, Ch. 5, pages 60–65
- Guide practice on Book Journal Entry 6

Independent Work
- Repeated Reading: Partner or Whisper Read, Flat Stanley, Ch. 5, pages 60–65
- Book Journal Entry 6

Homework
- Homework Passage 6

Day 9

Teacher-Directed
- Exercise 7
- Fluency, Prickly Penelope (Exercise 7b)

Independent Work
- Repeated Reading: Partner or Whisper Read, Fluency, Prickly Penelope (Exercise 7b)
- Written Assessment
- ORF Assessment*

Homework
- Homework Passage 7

10-, 11-, or 12-DAY PLAN • *Intervention*
For Days 1–9, follow 9-Day plan. Add Days 10, 11, 12 as follows:

Day 10 Extra Practice 1

Teacher-Directed
- Decoding Practice
- Fluency Passage

Independent Work
- Activity and Word Fluency A

Homework
- Fluency Passage

Day 11 Extra Practice 2

Teacher-Directed
- Decoding Practice
- Fluency Passage

Independent Work
- Activity and Word Fluency B

Homework
- Fluency Passage

Day 12 Extra Practice 3

Teacher-Directed
- Decoding Practice
- Fluency Passage

Independent Work
- Activity and Word Fluency A or B
- ORF Assessment*

Homework
- Fluency Passage

Materials and Materials Preparation

Core Lessons

Teacher Materials

READ WELL 2 MATERIALS

- Unit 19 Teacher's Guide
- Sound Cards
- Unit 19 Oral Reading Fluency Assessment found on page 116
- Group Assessment Record found in the *Assessment Manual*

SCHOOL SUPPLIES

Stopwatch or watch with a second hand

Student Materials

READ WELL 2 MATERIALS (for each student)

- *Flat Stanley*
- *Exercise Book 3*
- *Activity Book 3* or copies of Unit 19 Comprehension and Skill Work
- Unit 19 Written Assessment found in *Activity Book 3*, page 123, and on the blackline master CD
- Unit 19 Certificate of Achievement (BLM, page 117)
- Unit 19 Homework (blackline masters)
  See *Getting Started* for suggested homework routines.

SCHOOL SUPPLIES

Pencils, colors (optional—markers, crayons, or colored pencils)

> Make one copy per student of each blackline master, as appropriate for the group.
>
> *Note:* For new or difficult Comprehension and Skill Activities, make overhead transparencies from the blackline masters. Use the transparencies to demonstrate and guide practice.

Extra Practice Lessons

> **CAUTION**
> Use these lessons only if needed. Students who need Extra Practice may benefit from one, two, or three lessons.

Student Materials

READ WELL 2 MATERIALS (for each student, as needed)

See Extra Practice blackline masters located on the CD.
- Unit 19 Extra Practice 1: Decoding Practice, Fluency Passage, Word Fluency A, and Activity
- Unit 19 Extra Practice 2: Decoding Practice, Fluency Passage, Word Fluency B, and Activity
- Unit 19 Extra Practice 3: Decoding Practice, Fluency Passage, Word Fluency A or B, and Activity

SCHOOL SUPPLIES

Pencils, colors (optional—markers, crayons, or colored pencils), highlighters

Important Tips

Pacing: Achieving Grade Level and Above

		PACING CHART	
Theme	**Unit No.**	**Unit**	**Days in Core Plan**
Our World, Our Home	1	Maya and Ben	6
	2	Mapping Our World	6
	3	African Adventures	6
Communities	4	Arthur's Pet Business*	2
	5	Life as an Ant	6
	6	Sir Henry	6
	7	Stories from Hilo	6
From Generation to Generation	8	Traditional Tales	7
	9	Family Tales*	6
All About Dinosaurs	10	Dino Discoveries	6
	11	Dog Detective	6
	12	Dinosaurs Before Dark	10
Spiders and Bats	13	Spiders	8
	14	Bats	6
Young America	15	Snapshots of the American West	6
	16	Wild, Wild West	6
Interdependence	17	RW Science Digest Vol. 1: Food Chains	6
	18	The Reef	6
Imagination	19	Flat Stanley	7
	20	MSB: Inside the Human Body	6

* Review Unit

GRADE LEVEL

Grade level is not a standard concept and is determined in a variety of ways. Our field test results indicated that students scored at least a 3.0 in grade equivalence when completing Unit 19.

Many students scored higher (field test students scored, on average, a 3.7 grade equivalency on the Woodcock Reading Mastery Short Scale).

CELEBRATE!

You are here.

LOOKING AHEAD

Read Well 2 Plus continues moving your high-performing students forward. Your students will read a biography of Lincoln; *Read Well Science Digest Vol. 2*; and three great trade books: *Thomas Edison: A Brilliant Inventor, Judy Moody Saves the World!,* and *The Absent Author.*

Students and parents alike will be delighted as students:

- write their own Lincoln mini-book.
- complete a timeline about Edison.
- write their own Science Digest.
- write notes and letters to Judy Moody.
- complete a detective's case log.
- vote for their favorites with the *Read Well* Literary Awards.

Read Well Plus			Working Above Grade Level
Inspiring People	21	A Great Man	6
	22	Thomas Edison: A Brilliant Inventor	8
Earth We Share	23	RW Science Digest Vol. 2: Where in the World?	8
	24	Judy Moody Saves the World!	12
Mystery	25	The Absent Author	9

Note: If your students placed in *RW2* Unit 5 or higher at the beginning of the school year, you may find that you have additional time at the end of the school year to study another trade book of your choice.

How to Teach the Lessons

Teach from this section. Each instructional component is outlined in an easy-to-teach format.

Exercise 1

- Story Opener: Flat Stanley
- Vocabulary, Story Reading 1
  With the Teacher: Chapter 1
- Book Journal Cover, Entry 1, Comprehension and Skill Activity 1

Exercise 2

- Vocabulary, Story Reading 2
  With the Teacher: Chapter 2, pages 8–15
  On Your Own: Chapter 2, pages 16–21
- Book Journal Entry 2, Comprehension and Skill Activity 2

Exercise 3

- Vocabulary, Story Reading 3
  With the Teacher: Chapter 3, pages 22–27
  On Your Own: Chapter 3, pages 28–33
- Book Journal Entry 3, Comprehension and Skill Activity 3

Exercise 4

- Vocabulary, Story Reading 4
  With the Teacher: Chapter 4, pages 34–39
  On Your Own: Chapter 4, pages 39–45
- Book Journal Entry 4, Comprehension and Skill Activity 4

Exercise 5

- Vocabulary, Story Reading 5
  With the Teacher: Chapter 4, pages 46–49
  On Your Own: Chapter 4, pages 49–53
- Book Journal Entry 5, Comprehension and Skill Activity 5

Exercise 6

- Vocabulary, Story Reading 6
  With the Teacher: Chapter 5, pages 54–60
  On Your Own: Chapter 5, pages 60–65
- Book Journal Entry 6, Comprehension and Skill Activity 6

Exercise 7

- Story Reading 7
  With the Teacher: Prickly Penelope (Fluency, Exercise 7b)
- Written Assessment

Note: Lessons include daily homework.

❶ SOUND REVIEW

Use selected Sound Cards from Units 1–18.

PACING

Exercise 1 should take about 15 minutes.

❷ SHIFTY WORD BLENDING

For each word, have students say the underlined sound. Then have them sound out the word smoothly and say it. Use the words in sentences, as appropriate.

❸ ACCURACY AND FLUENCY BUILDING

B2. Reading by Analogy

Have students figure out how to read "measurement" by reading other words they know.

BUILD ACCURACY AND FLUENCY (Reminder)

For all rows and columns, follow the specific directions, then build accuracy and fluency with whole words.

C1. Multisyllabic Words

• For the list of words divided by syllables, have students read each syllable, then the whole word. Use the word in a sentence, as appropriate.

• For the list of whole words, build accuracy and then fluency.

darndest	My brother likes to clean all day. Isn't that the . . . *darndest* . . . thing!
bulletin	The class rules are posted on the . . . *bulletin* . . . board.
absurd	Something that is ridiculous is . . . *absurd.*
Lambchop	The man's name was Mr. . . . *Lambchop.*

E1. Tricky Words

• For each Tricky Word, have students use the sounds and word parts they know to silently sound out the word. Use the word in a sentence to help with pronunciation.

• If the word is unfamiliar, tell students the word.

younger

Look at the first word. You already know part of this word. Read the small word. (young)
Now read the whole word. (younger) My little sister is . . . *younger* . . . than I am.
Read the word three times. (younger, younger, younger)

brother's	That is not Sissy's coat. That is her . . . *brother's* . . . coat.
clothes	With her birthday money, Mariah is going to buy new . . . *clothes.*

• Have students go back and read the whole words in the column.

❹ WORDS IN CONTEXT

For each word, have students use the sounds and word parts they know to silently sound out the word. Then have students read the sentence. Assist, as needed.

❺ MORPHOGRAPHS AND AFFIXES

• For Row A, say something like:

Look at the first word. Read the underlined part. (be) Now read the word. (believe)
Look at the next word. Read the underlined part. (able) Read the word. (believable)
When something is *believable*, we are able to believe it. Look at the next word.
Read the underlined part. (un) Read the word. (unbelievable) What does *un-* mean? (not)
So *unbelievable* means we are *not* able to believe it.

• For Rows B and C, have students read the underlined part, then the word.

• Repeat practice with whole words, mixing group and individual turns. Build accuracy, then fluency.

❻ GENERALIZATION: READING NEW WORDS IN PARAGRAPHS

- Have students read the paragraph silently, then out loud. Tell students to use the sounds and word parts they know to read any difficult words.
- Repeat practice, as needed.

Flat Stanley

Unit 19 Exercise 1
Use before Chapter 1

1. SOUND REVIEW Use selected Sound Cards from Units 1–18.

2. SHIFTY WORD BLENDING For each word, have students say the underlined part, sound out smoothly, then read the word.

| sh<u>out</u> | sh<u>ee</u>t | shee<u>p</u> | <u>sl</u>eep | <u>sl</u>eep<u>ing</u> |

3. ACCURACY/FLUENCY BUILDING For each column, have students say any underlined part, then read each word. Next, have them read the column.

A1 **Mixed Practice**	B1 **Related Words**	C1 **Multisyllabic Words**	D1 **Word Endings**	E1 **Tricky Words**
h<u>ay</u>	examine	darn·dest	<u>doctors</u>	younger
off<u>ice</u>	examined	bul·le·tin	<u>altered</u>	brother's
mar<u>v</u>el	examination	ab·surd	<u>heavens</u>	clothes
p<u>o</u>lite	**B2** **Reading by Analogy**	Lamb·chop	<u>training</u>	
p<u>oi</u>nted	treasure	darndest	<u>woken</u>	
n<u>ur</u>se	measure	bulletin	tickle	
	measurement	absurd	tickly	
		Lambchop		

4. WORDS IN CONTEXT Have students use the sounds and word parts they know to figure out each word. Then have them read each sentence.

| Ⓐ | mes·sa·ges | My husband left ten <u>messages</u> on my phone. |
| Ⓑ | ex·per·i·ence | Getting lost was the worst <u>experience</u> of Arthur's life. |

5. MORPHOGRAPHS AND AFFIXES Have students read the underlined part, then the word.

Ⓐ	<u>bel</u>ieve	believ<u>able</u>	<u>un</u>believable	
Ⓑ	enorm<u>ous</u>	<u>ex</u>cuse	tail<u>or</u>	polite<u>ness</u>
Ⓒ	<u>de</u>spite	<u>be</u>neath	care<u>ful</u>	cheerful<u>ly</u>

6. GENERALIZATION Have students read the paragraph silently, then out loud. (New words: Stanley, Christmas, snowboard, ripped)

Stanley was so excited! It was Christmas day, and he just knew he was going to get a snowboard. He had asked for one last year, but his mom said it was too expensive. The family gathered around the tree as Dad handed out the presents. He handed Stanley a large package. Stanley ripped it open and there it was—the snowboard he'd been hoping for!

TEAM EXPECTATIONS (Reminder)

Have students tell you the team expectations. Say something like:
Who can tell me the first two team rules?

1. Sit up.
2. Follow directions.
3. Help each other.
4. Work hard and have fun.

GENERALIZATION (Reminder)

The generalization task provides an opportunity for you to informally assess students' ability to read new words that have not been pretaught.

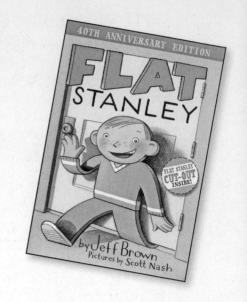

COMPREHENSION PROCESSES

Remember, Understand, Apply

PROCEDURES

1. **Introducing the Storybook**

   Viewing; Identifying—Title, Main Characters, Author; Inferring; Using Vocabulary—popular

   Have students identify the title of their new storybook.

   Say something like:

   Everyone, look at the cover of the book.

   What's the title of this book? (Flat Stanley)

   The main characters in the story are Stanley and Arthur.

   Who are the main characters? (Stanley and Arthur)

   Who is the author? (Jeff Brown)

   Jeff Brown, like Mary Pope Osborne, is a popular author of children's books.

   Why do you think Jeff Brown is a popular author?

2. Working With the Table of Contents

Identifying—Title; Inferring; Predicting

Have students look at the Table of Contents. Say something like:

How many chapters are in the book? (five)

What's the name of the first chapter?
(The Big Bulletin Board)

What page does it begin on? (one)

Sometimes the chapter titles give you clues about the story. Where do you think Chapter 1 is going to take place?

(It will take place in a school with a bulletin board . . .)

Glance through the chapter titles.

> **THINK ALOUD WITH YOUR STUDENTS**
>
> Say things like:
> When we say someone is *flat*, it sometimes means they are unhappy. I wonder if Stanley is going to be unhappy in Chapter 2. What do you think?

What else can you predict about the book?
(Stanley is going to be flat. There's going to be a robbery at the museum . . .)

CONTENTS

1. The Big Bulletin Board 1

2. Being Flat 9

3. Stanley the Kite 23

4. The Museum Thieves 35

5. Arthur's Good Idea 55

COMPREHENSION PROCESSES

Understand, Apply

PROCEDURES

Introducing Vocabulary

> ☆polite ☆politeness, examine, despite ☆marvel ☆alter ☆absurd

- For each vocabulary word, have students read the word by parts, then read the whole word.
- Read the student-friendly explanations to students as they follow with their fingers. Then have students use the vocabulary word by following the gray text.
- Review and discuss the illustrations.

Note: Student vocabulary pages for this unit are found in the students' *Exercise Book 3*.

USING VOCABULARY

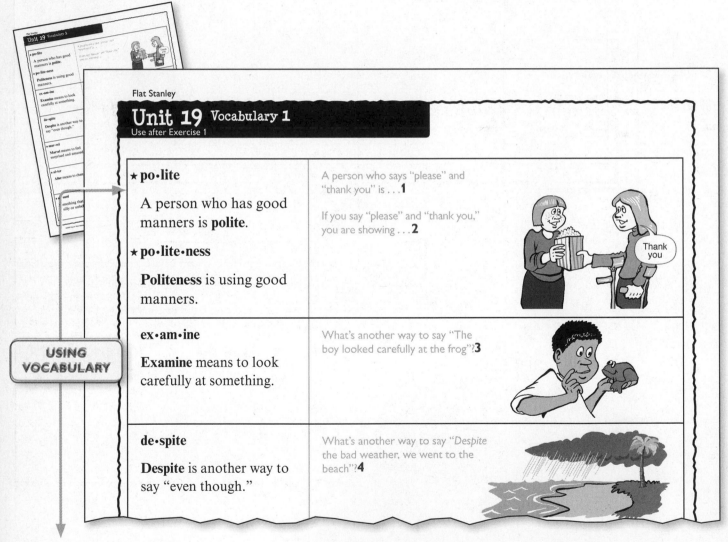

Flat Stanley

Unit 19 Vocabulary 1
Use after Exercise 1

★ **po·lite**	A person who says "please" and "thank you" is . . . **1**
A person who has good manners is **polite**.	If you say "please" and "thank you," you are showing . . . **2**
★ **po·lite·ness**	
Politeness is using good manners.	
ex·am·ine	What's another way to say "The boy looked carefully at the frog"?**3**
Examine means to look carefully at something.	
de·spite	What's another way to say "*Despite* the bad weather, we went to the beach"?**4**
Despite is another way to say "even though."	

❶ **Understand:** Using Vocabulary—polite (polite)

❷ **Apply:** Using Vocabulary—politeness (politeness)

❸ **Apply:** Using Vocabulary—examine (The boy examined the frog.)

❹ **Apply:** Using Vocabulary—despite (Even though the weather was bad, we went to the beach.)

☆ = New in this unit

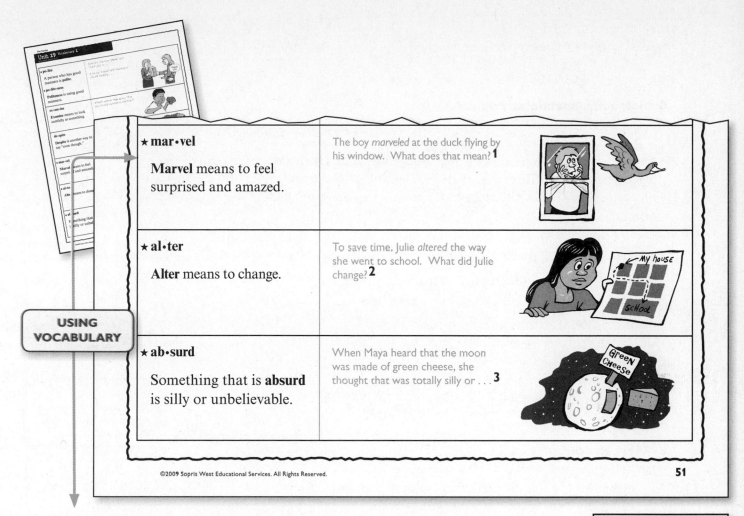

51

❶ **Understand:** Defining and Using Vocabulary—marvel (The boy was surprised and amazed by the duck.)

❷ **Apply:** Using Vocabulary—alter (Julie changed the way she went to school.)

❸ **Understand:** Using Vocabulary—absurd (absurd)

USING VOCABULARY

Be enthusiastic about learning new words. Keep a running list of words you would like to use and encourage students to use. Keep the list handy when you are teaching. Put students' names on the board to acknowledge use of a word. Say things like:

Wow! [Cesar] used the word *absurd* when he talked about the movie he saw last night.

19

CHAPTER 1 INSTRUCTIONS
Students read Chapter 1 with the teacher.

COMPREHENSION PROCESSES
Remember, Understand, Apply, Analyze

COMPREHENSION BUILDING
- Encourage students to answer questions with complete sentences.
- If students have difficulty comprehending, think aloud with them or reread the portion of the story that answers the question. Repeat the question.

PROCEDURES

1. **Introducing Chapter 1**

   Viewing; Inferring; Identifying—Title
   Discuss the main picture. Say something like:
   Turn to page 1. Look at the picture. Can you tell where this chapter takes place?
   (It takes place in Stanley's house . . .)
   What do you think the boy is doing? (He's calling for someone . . .)
   Have students read the title.
   What's the title of Chapter 1? (The Big Bulletin Board)
   I wonder if Stanley has a bulletin board in his house. That's kind of fun.

   > **CORRECTING DECODING ERRORS**
   >
   > During story reading, gently correct any error, then have students reread the sentence.

2. **First Reading**
   - Ask questions and discuss the story as indicated by the blue text in this guide.
   - Mix group and individual turns, independent of your voice.
     Have students work toward a group accuracy goal of 0–4 errors.
     Quietly keep track of errors made by all students in the group.
   - After reading the story, practice any difficult words.
     Reread the story if students have not reached the accuracy goal.

3. **Second Reading, Short Passage Practice: Developing Prosody**
   - Demonstrate expressive, fluent reading of the first paragraph. Read at a rate slightly faster than the students' rate.
   - Guide practice with your voice.
   - Provide individual turns while others track with their fingers and whisper read.
   - Repeat with one paragraph at a time.

   > **REPEATED READINGS**
   > **Prosody**
   >
   > On the second reading, students practice developing prosody—phrasing and expression. Research has shown that prosody is related to both fluency and comprehension.

4. **Partner or Whisper Reading: Repeated Reading**

    Before beginning independent work, have students finger track and partner or whisper read.

5. **Comprehension and Skill Work**
   For students on a 7-Day Plan, tell them they will do Activity 1 and start their Book Journal after they read Chapter 1. Guide practice, as needed. For teacher directions, see pages 25–27. (For 9- to 12-Day Plans, see the Lesson Planner, page 9.)

6. **Homework 1: New Passage**

THE BIG BULLETIN BOARD

Breakfast was ready.

"I will go wake the boys," Mrs. Lambchop said to her husband, George Lambchop. Just then their younger son, Arthur, called from the bedroom he shared with his brother, Stanley.

"Hey! Come and look! Hey!"

1

After Reading Page 1

❶ **Remember:** Identifying—What
What did Arthur call out?
(Hey! Come and look! Hey!)

❷ **Apply:** Inferring; Using Vocabulary—ordinary
Do you think this is going to be an ordinary day?
(no)

❸ **Apply:** Inferring, Explaining, Viewing
Why do you think it's not going to be an ordinary day?
(Arthur is calling for his parents to come see something. He looks excited.)

Mr. and Mrs. Lambchop were both very much in favor of politeness and careful speech. "Hay is for horses, Arthur, not people," Mr. Lambchop said as they entered the bedroom. "Try to remember that."

"Excuse me," Arthur said. "But look!"

He pointed to Stanley's bed. Across it lay the enormous bulletin board that Mr. Lambchop had given the boys a Christmas ago so that they could pin up pictures and messages and maps. It had fallen, during the night, on top of Stanley.

But Stanley was not hurt. In fact, he would still have been sleeping if he had not been woken by his brother's shout.

"What's going on here?" he called out cheerfully from beneath the enormous board.

2

After Reading Page 2

❶ **Apply:** Inferring, Explaining
Why did Mr. Lambchop say, "Hay is for horses"?
(He didn't like Arthur to call him by saying "hey" instead of using his name.)

❷ **Remember:** Identifying—Event
What happened to Stanley during the night?
(A bulletin board fell on him.)

❸ **Understand:** Explaining
What does the book say that makes us know Stanley is fine?
(It says he wasn't hurt. It says Stanley called out "cheerfully" from beneath the bulletin board.)

❹ **Apply:** Viewing, Inferring, Explaining
Look at the picture. What's odd about Stanley?
(He's flat.)

Mr. and Mrs. Lambchop hurried to lift it from the bed.

"Heavens!" said Mrs. Lambchop.

"Gosh!" said Arthur. "Stanley's flat!"

"As a pancake," said Mr. Lambchop. "Darndest thing I've ever seen."

"Let's all have breakfast," Mrs. Lambchop said. "Then Stanley and I will go see Dr. Dan and hear what he has to say."

In his office, Dr. Dan examined Stanley all over.

"How do you feel?" he asked. "Does it hurt very much?"

"I felt sort of tickly for a while after I got up," Stanley Lambchop said, "but I feel fine now."

4

After Reading Page 4

❶ **Apply:** Inferring, Explaining
Why did Mr. Lambchop say, "Darndest thing I've ever seen"?
(Stanley was flat, and that's very unusual.)

❷ **Apply:** Inferring; Explaining; Using Vocabulary—absurd
Why is it totally silly, or absurd, that Mrs. Lambchop said, "Let's all have breakfast," before taking Stanley to the doctor?
(She should be worried and take Stanley to the doctor right away.)

❸ **Understand:** Visualizing, Describing; **Apply:** Making Connections
Close your eyes. Imagine being as flat as a pancake. What would it be like?
(It would feel very strange. It would feel like you were light and could blow away . . . It would be weird!)

"Well, that's mostly how it is with these cases," said Dr. Dan.

"We'll just have to keep an eye on this young fellow," he said when he had finished the examination. "Sometimes we doctors, despite all our years of training and experience, can only marvel at how little we really know."

Mrs. Lambchop said she thought Stanley's clothes would have to be altered by the tailor now, so Dr. Dan told his nurse to take Stanley's measurements.

Mrs. Lambchop wrote them down.

Stanley was four feet tall, about a foot wide, and half an inch thick.

After Reading Page 6

❶ **Analyze:** Inferring; **Understand:** Explaining
Why do you think Dr. Dan said, "Sometimes we doctors, despite all our years of training and experience, can only marvel at how little we really know"?
(Stanley was flat, and that's very unusual. Dr. Dan didn't know what to think—even though he is a doctor.)

FOCUS ON COMPARING AND CONTRASTING

Using Vocabulary— approximately

After completing the page, compare Stanley's measurements with a student in your group. Say something like:
How tall was Stanley? (four feet tall)
Let's measure [Tomas].
How tall is [Tomas]? (four feet and one inch)
So, we can say [Tomas] is *approximately* four feet tall. Are Thomas and Stanley about the same height? (yes)

How wide is Stanley? (a foot wide)
How wide is [Tomas]? (approximately a foot wide)
So, Stanley and [Tomas] are about the same width.

How thick is Stanley? (about a half inch thick)
How thick is [Tomas]? (approximately 8 inches thick)
So, are Stanley and [Tomas] about the same thickness? (no, absolutely not)
Stanley is absurdly thin!

COVER PAGE

COMPREHENSION PROCESSES
Remember, Understand

WRITING TRAITS
Conventions—Capital, Period
Presentation

Illustrating →

Locating Information; Identifying—
Title, Author, Illustrator →

PROCEDURES
Discuss each step. Then have students complete the page independently.

1. Book Journal: Introduction
Remind students that a book journal is a place to write down how we feel and think about the story. Say something like:
Read the title. (My Book Journal)
A book journal is made up of your personal thoughts and feelings about what the author has written.

After reading each chapter of *Flat Stanley*, you will have a chance to write something about what you just read. What you write in the journal is called an entry.

2. Cover: Locating and Filling in Information—Specific Instructions
• Have students identify what they will write on each line of the cover. Say something like:
Today, one of your jobs is to begin creating the cover.
Touch where you will write the title of the book. Remember, you'll need a capital at the beginning of each word, except for little words like *a* and *the* in the middle of the title.
Does this title have any little words? (no)
Which words begin with a capital? (all the words)
Touch where you'll write the author's name.
How will you know how to spell Jeff Brown's name? (Look at the book.)
Can you find the illustrator's name on the cover? (Scott Nash)

• Have students illustrate a scene from the story after they've read more of the book.
What does the first line say? (Cover art by . . .) That's right. The cover art is going to be by *you*.
Cover art is very important because its purpose is to get new readers interested in the book.
I'm going to have you read more of the book so you can decide what you want to draw.
For now, write your name after "Cover art by . . . "

Unit 19   Use after Exercise 1 and Chapter 1

Entry 1 (1 of 2)

My Book Journal

Cover art by: _Minnie Bird_

Title of book: _Flat Stanley_

Author: _Jeff Brown_

Illustrator: _Scott Nash_

(Teachers: If you are using the Activity Book, tear out and staple pages 73 to 80 to make a separate Book Journal.)

©2009 Sopris West Educational Services. All Rights Reserved.   73

ENTRY 1

COMPREHENSION PROCESSES

Remember, Understand, Apply, Create

WRITING TRAITS

Ideas and Content
Word Choice
Conventions—Complete Sentence,
Capital, Period
Presentation

      Identifying—Main Character

Using Graphic Organizer; Describing—
    Character Traits (Characterization)
                 Illustrating

Generating Ideas; Using Vocabulary—
        speechless, distressed

PROCEDURES

For each step, demonstrate and guide
practice, as needed. Then have students
complete the page independently.

1. **Main Character: Answering
   Question** (Item 1)

2. **Characterization: Web,
   Illustrating—Specific
   Instructions** (Item 2)
   - Have students write words
     or phrases that describe
     the character.
   - Have students draw a picture of the character.

3. **Personal Response: Creative Writing—Specific Instructions**
   - Have students write a paragraph about what they would do if they woke up flat as
     a pancake.
   - Think aloud with students and have students brainstorm possible answers with partners.
     Say something like:
     Look at the sign that the bird is holding. Read it.
     (Try to use a snazzy word: distressed, speechless, amazed)
     [Jasmine], what does *speechless* mean? (You are so surprised, you can't talk.)
     Yes, so I could use that snazzy word and complete the sentence. "If I woke up as flat as a
     pancake, I would be surprised and speechless."
     Read the next directions. (Write two things you would do if you were as flat as a pancake . . .)
     Let's see. I think I would see if I could stand up. Then I think I would do a little dance to see if
     I was okay. So my answer would read, "If I woke up as flat as a pancake, I would be speechless.
     First I would stand up. Then I would do a little dance to see if I was okay."

     Partner 1, tell Partner 2 what you might write.
     Partner 2, tell Partner 1 what you might write.

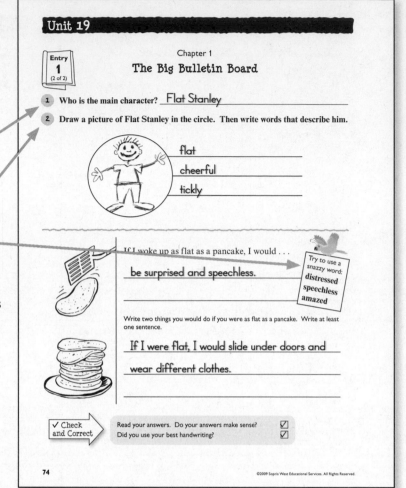

STORY COMPREHENSION

COMPREHENSION PROCESSES

Remember, Understand, Apply, Analyze

Identifying—Character Traits (Characterization)

Using Graphic Organizer, Distinguishing Cause/Effect

Identifying—What

Identifying—Character Traits (Characterization), Locating Information

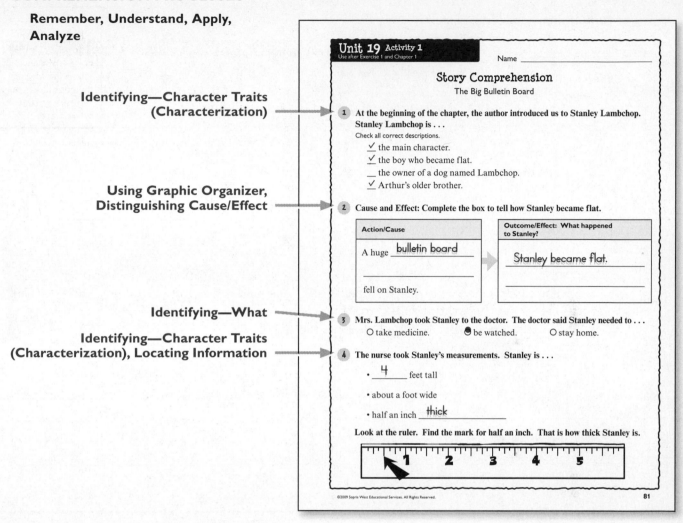

Unit 19 Activity 1
Use after Exercise 1 and Chapter 1

Name _____

Story Comprehension
The Big Bulletin Board

1. At the beginning of the chapter, the author introduced us to Stanley Lambchop. Stanley Lambchop is . . .
   Check all correct descriptions.
   ✓ the main character.
   ✓ the boy who became flat.
   ___ the owner of a dog named Lambchop.
   ✓ Arthur's older brother.

2. Cause and Effect: Complete the box to tell how Stanley became flat.

Action/Cause	Outcome/Effect: What happened to Stanley?
A huge _bulletin board_ fell on Stanley.	Stanley became flat.

3. Mrs. Lambchop took Stanley to the doctor. The doctor said Stanley needed to . . .
   ○ take medicine.   ● be watched.   ○ stay home.

4. The nurse took Stanley's measurements. Stanley is . . .
   • __4__ feet tall
   • about a foot wide
   • half an inch _thick_

   Look at the ruler. Find the mark for half an inch. That is how thick Stanley is.

       81

PROCEDURES

For each step, demonstrate and guide practice, as needed. Then have students complete the page independently.

1. **Selection Response—Basic Instructions** (Items 1, 3)
   Have students read the sentence starters, then fill in the bubble or check the blanks with the correct answer.

2. **Cause and Effect: Sequence Chart, Sentence Completion—Specific Instructions** (Item 2)
   Have students read the directions and complete the chart.

3. **Characterization: Answering Questions—Specific Instructions** (Item 4)
   Have students fill in Stanley's measurements. Remind them to look back in their book if they need to.

Self-monitoring
Have students check and correct their work.

❶ SOUND REVIEW

Have students read the sounds and key word phrases. Work for accuracy, then fluency.

❷ ACCURACY AND FLUENCY BUILDING

C1. Multisyllabic Words

- For the list of words divided by syllables, have students read each syllable, then the whole word. Use the word in a sentence, as appropriate.
- For the list of whole words, build accuracy and then fluency.

limber	Dancers can move and bend easily. They are . . . *limber.*
envelope	The woman put the letter in an . . . *envelope.*
apologized	Mel was sorry, so he . . . *apologized.*
Jeffreys	My neighbors are the . . . *Jeffreys.*
recently	They went to town a little while ago. They went . . . *recently.*
favorite	I like chocolate ice cream the best. What flavor is your . . . *favorite?*
vacation	The Lambchops are going to Arizona for their . . . *vacation.*

D1. Tricky Words

- For each Tricky Word, have students use the sounds and word parts they know to silently sound out the word. Use the word in a sentence to help with pronunciation.
- If the word is unfamiliar, tell students the word.

cuckoo
Look at the first word. Say the word parts silently. Thumbs up when you know the word.
Use my sentence to help you pronounce the word. You might say a silly person is . . . *cuckoo.*
Read the word three times. (cuckoo, cuckoo, cuckoo)

insurance
Look at the next word. Say the word parts silently. Thumbs up when you know the word.
Use my sentence to help you pronounce the word. To drive a car, you need . . . *insurance.*
Read the word three times. (insurance, insurance, insurance)

straightened	Lauren got her curly hair . . . *straightened.*
proved	Ann's friends didn't think she could do a backflip. She . . . *proved . . .* she could do it.
California	Los Angeles is in the state of . . . *California.*
caught	I tossed the ball to Pedro. He . . . *caught . . .* it.

- Have students go back and read the whole words in the column.

❸ WORD ENDINGS

Have students read any underlined word, then the word with an ending.

❹ WORDS IN CONTEXT

For each word, have students use the sounds and word parts they know to silently sound out the word. Then have students read the sentence. Assist, as needed.

❺ MORPHOGRAPHS AND AFFIXES

★Have students practice reading *in-* and the related words.
- For Row B, have students read the underlined part, then the whole word.

★ = New in this unit

28

❻ GENERALIZATION: READING NEW WORDS IN PARAGRAPHS
- Have students read the paragraph silently, then out loud. Tell students to use the sounds and word parts they know to read any difficult words.
- Repeat practice, as needed.

Flat Stanley

Unit 19 Exercise 2
Use before Chapter 2

1. SOUND REVIEW Have students review sounds for accuracy, then for fluency.

A	-y as in fly	ow as in cow	a as in ago	au as in astronaut	o_e as in bone
B	igh	i_e	aw	or	oi

2. ACCURACY/FLUENCY BUILDING For each column, have students say any underlined part, then read each word. Next, have them read the column.

A1 Mixed Practice	B1 Related Words	C1 Multisyllabic Words		D1 Tricky Words
ma̲r̲kings	angry	lim·ber	limber	cuckoo
la̲c̲es	anger	en·ve·lope	envelope	insurance
fragi̲l̲e	angrily	a·pol·o·gized	apologized	straightened
v̲oi̲ce		Jef·freys	Jeffreys	proved
br̲ea̲d		re·cent·ly	recently	California
lad̲y̲		fa·vor·ite	favorite	caught
r̲u̲de		va·ca·tion	vacation	
tw̲ice̲				

3. WORD ENDINGS Have students read any underlined word, then the word with an ending.

A	lower̲ed̲	letter̲ed̲	handl̲ed̲	bang̲ed̲
B	grate grating	slide sliding	haste hasty	rap rapped

4. WORDS IN CONTEXT For each word, have students use the sounds and word parts they know to figure out the word. Then have them read the sentence.

A	jeal·ous	Anthony was <u>jealous</u> of Thomas because he had a new yo-yo.
B	Post·al Ser·vice	The <u>Postal Service</u> didn't deliver my postcard. I forgot stamps.
C	ly·ing	I knew my dog was probably just <u>lying</u> around someplace.

5. MORPHOGRAPHS AND AFFIXES Have students practice reading "in-" and the related words. For Row B, have students read the underlined part, then the word.

A	★in-	<u>in</u>sert	<u>in</u>vited	<u>in</u>deed	<u>in</u>side
B	sharp<u>ly</u>	<u>re</u>marks	nerv<u>ous</u>	flex<u>ible</u>	valu<u>able</u>

6. GENERALIZATION Have students read the paragraph silently, then out loud. (New words: Harry, policeman, ticket)

Harry wants to be a policeman when he grows up, just like his dad. One time, Harry's dad had to give a friend a speeding ticket. He said sometimes being a policeman could be hard. But he told Harry you have to have integrity. Harry looks up to his dad and respects him.

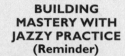

> **BUILDING MASTERY WITH JAZZY PRACTICE (Reminder)**
>
> For variety, practice underlined sounds in a jazzy rhythm. Say something like: Listen to me read Column A1 in a rhythm. I'm going to quickly say each underlined sound two times and then read the word.
>
> /ar/, /ar/, markings;
> /sss/, /sss/, laces
> /j/, /j/, fragile . . .
>
> Your turn. Start at the top of Column A1 and keep going.
>
> (/ar/, /ar/, markings;
> /sss/, /sss/, laces
> /j/, /j/, fragile . . .)

COMPREHENSION PROCESSES

Understand, Apply

PROCEDURES

Introducing Vocabulary

★ jealous ★ hasty ★ recently ★ round-trip ★ limber, valuable ★ fragile

• For each vocabulary word, have students read the word by parts, then read the whole word.
• Read the student-friendly explanations to students as they follow with their fingers. Then have students use the vocabulary word by following the gray text.
• Review and discuss the illustrations.
  Note: Student vocabulary pages for this unit are found in the students' *Exercise Book 3*.

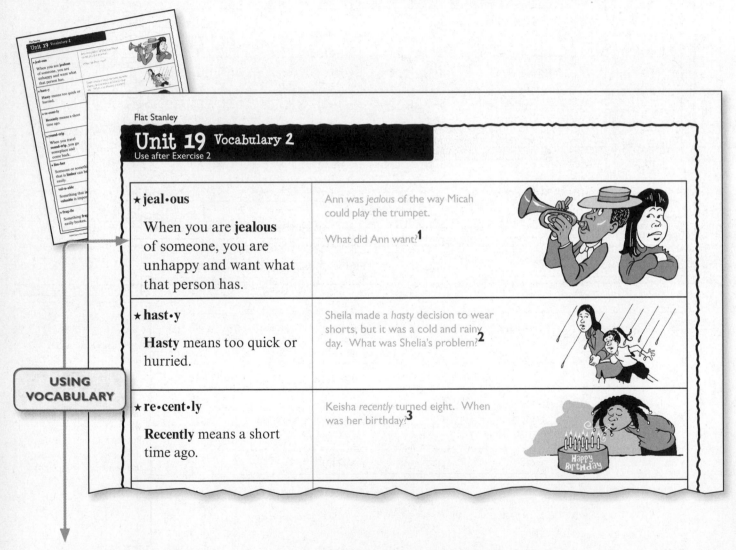

USING VOCABULARY

Flat Stanley

Unit 19 Vocabulary 2
Use after Exercise 2

★ jeal•ous When you are **jealous** of someone, you are unhappy and want what that person has.	Ann was *jealous* of the way Micah could play the trumpet. What did Ann want?[1]
★ hast•y **Hasty** means too quick or hurried.	Sheila made a *hasty* decision to wear shorts, but it was a cold and rainy day. What was Shelia's problem?[2]
★ re•cent•ly **Recently** means a short time ago.	Keisha *recently* turned eight. When was her birthday?[3]

❶ **Apply:** Using Vocabulary—jealous (Ann wanted to play the trumpet as well as Micah.)

❷ **Apply:** Using Vocabulary—hasty (She was dressed wrong because she made a hasty decision.)

❸ **Understand:** Using Vocabulary—recently (Keisha's birthday was a short time ago.)

★ = New in this unit

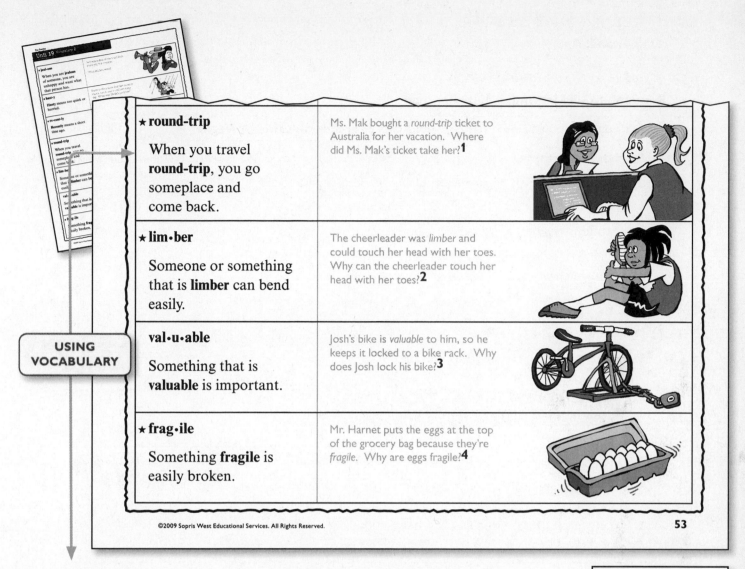

USING VOCABULARY

★ **round-trip**	Ms. Mak bought a *round-trip* ticket to Australia for her vacation. Where did Ms. Mak's ticket take her?[1]	
When you travel **round-trip**, you go someplace and come back.		
★ **lim•ber**	The cheerleader was *limber* and could touch her head with her toes. Why can the cheerleader touch her head with her toes?[2]	
Someone or something that is **limber** can bend easily.		
val•u•able	Josh's bike is *valuable* to him, so he keeps it locked to a bike rack. Why does Josh lock his bike?[3]	
Something that is **valuable** is important.		
★ **frag•ile**	Mr. Harnet puts the eggs at the top of the grocery bag because they're *fragile*. Why are eggs fragile?[4]	
Something **fragile** is easily broken.		

53

❶ **Apply:** Using Vocabulary—round-trip (Ms. Mak's round-trip ticket took her to Australia and back.)

❷ **Understand:** Using Vocabulary—limber (The cheerleader can touch her head with her toes because she is limber.)

❸ **Understand:** Using Vocabulary—valuable (Josh locks his bike because it is valuable to him. He doesn't want it stolen.)

❹ **Understand:** Defining and Using Vocabulary—fragile (Eggs are fragile because they break easily.)

USING VOCABULARY

Be enthusiastic about learning new words. Keep a running list of words you would like to use and encourage students to use. Keep the list handy when you are teaching. Put students' names on the board to acknowledge use of a word. Say things like:

Wow! [Jamie] used the word *recently* when he was talking about morning recess.

CHAPTER 2 INSTRUCTIONS
Students read pages 8–15 with the teacher and pages 16–21 on their own.

COMPREHENSION PROCESSES
Remember, Understand, Apply, Analyze

PROCEDURES

1. Reviewing Chapter 1

Summarizing; Identifying—What; Using Vocabulary—absurd
Discuss Chapter 1. Say something like:
What was absurd or unbelievable in Chapter 1?
(Stanley was as flat as a pancake, and he was still okay.)
What did Dr. Dan think they should do?
(He thought they should keep an eye on Stanley.)
How thick was Stanley? (He was half an inch thick.)

2. Introducing Chapter 2

Identifying—Title; Viewing; Predicting
What's the title of this chapter? (Being Flat)
Look at the picture. What do you think is going to happen in Chapter 2?
(Stanley will stay flat. Stanley will have interesting experiences as a flat
person . . .)

3. First Reading
- Ask questions and discuss the story as indicated by the blue text in
  this guide.
- Mix group and individual turns, independent of your voice.
  Have students work toward a group accuracy goal of 0–5 errors.
  Quietly keep track of errors made by all students in the group.
- After reading the story, practice any difficult words.
  Reread the story if students have not reached the accuracy goal.

4. Second Reading, Timed Readings: Repeated Reading
- As time allows, have students do Timed Readings while others
  follow along.
- Time individuals for 30 seconds and encourage each child to
  work for a personal best.
- Determine words correct per minute. Record student scores.

BEING FLAT

When Stanley got used to being flat, he enjoyed it. He could go in and out of rooms, even when the door was closed, just by lying down and sliding through the crack at the bottom.

Mr. and Mrs. Lambchop said it was silly, but they were quite proud of him.

9

After Reading Page 9

❶ **Remember:** Identifying—How
How did Stanley feel about being flat?
(He liked being flat.)

❷ **Analyze:** Distinguishing Cause/Effect;
Apply: Explaining
What amazing thing could Stanley do because he was flat? (He could slide under the door.)

❸ **Analyze:** Drawing Conclusions
What else do you think was good about being flat?
(Stanley's parents were proud of him. He got attention. He was different . . .)

Arthur got jealous and tried to slide under a door, but he just banged his head.

Being flat could also be helpful, Stanley found.

He was taking a walk with Mrs. Lambchop one afternoon when her favorite ring fell from her finger. The ring rolled across the sidewalk and down between the bars of a grating that covered a deep, dark shaft. Mrs. Lambchop began to cry.

"I have an idea," Stanley said.

He took the laces out of his shoes and an extra pair out of his pocket and tied them all together to make one long lace. Then he tied one end of that to the back of his belt and gave the other end to his mother.

10

After Reading Page 10

❶ **Understand:** Defining and Using Vocabulary—
jealous
The book says Arthur was jealous. What does that mean?
(He was unhappy and wanted to be flat like Stanley.)

❷ **Understand:** Explaining—Problem
Mrs. Lambchop began to cry. What was her problem? (She dropped her ring, and it rolled where she couldn't get it.)

❸ **Apply:** Viewing, Inferring, **Understand:**
Explaining—Solution
Look at the picture. How is Stanley solving the problem?
(He's going down into the gutter to get the ring.)

Before Reading Page 12

❶ Apply: Viewing, Inferring, Explaining
Look at the picture. What is Mrs. Lambchop doing?
(She is holding Stanley by a string.)

❷ Analyze: Drawing Conclusions
The police officer looks concerned. Why do you
think he has his hands on his hips?
(He can't figure out what Mrs. Lambchop is
doing . . .)

"Lower me," he said, "and I will look for
the ring."

"Thank you, Stanley," Mrs. Lambchop
said. She lowered him between the bars and
moved him carefully up and down and from
side to side, so that he could search the
whole floor of the shaft.

Two policemen came by and stared at Mrs.
Lambchop as she stood holding the long lace
that ran down through the grating. She
pretended not to notice them.

"What's the matter, lady?" the first policeman asked. "Is your yo-yo stuck?"

"I am not playing with a yo-yo!" Mrs.
Lambchop said sharply. "My son is at the
other end of this lace, if you must know."

"Get the net, Harry," said the second

12

policeman. "We have caught a cuckoo!"

Just then, down in the shaft, Stanley cried out, "Hooray!"

Mrs. Lambchop pulled him up and saw that he had the ring.

"Good for you, Stanley," she said. Then she turned angrily to the policemen.

"A cuckoo, indeed!" she said. "Shame!"

The policemen apologized. "We didn't get it, lady," they said. "We have been hasty. We see that now."

"People should think twice before making rude remarks," said Mrs. Lambchop. "And then not make them at all."

The policemen realized that was a good rule and said they would try to remember it.

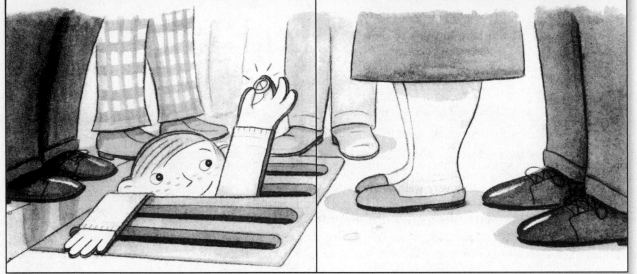

After Reading Page 14

❶ **Apply:** Inferring, Explaining
Why did the police officer think
Mrs. Lambchop was a cuckoo?
(She said her son was at the end of the
shoelace, and they thought she was crazy.)

After Reading Page 15

❶ **Apply:** Inferring, Explaining
Why did the police officer apologize to
Mrs. Lambchop?
(She wasn't cuckoo. Stanley really was at the end of
the shoelace.)

CHAPTER 2 INSTRUCTIONS

Students read pages 16–21 without the teacher, independently or
with partners.

COMPREHENSION PROCESSES

Remember, Understand, Evaluate

PROCEDURES

1. Getting Ready

Have students turn to page 16.

2. Setting a Purpose

Inferring; Explaining; Defining and Using Vocabulary—absurd

Before beginning reading, say something like:

The rest of this chapter is about another absurd event in Stanley's life. Things
are absurd when they are . . . silly and unbelievable.

As you read the next pages, try to answer:

- What did Stanley do that was absurd?
- Why was Mrs. Lampchop nervous?
- Why was it awesome to be flat?

PREP NOTE

Setting a Purpose

Write questions on a
chalkboard, white board,
or large piece of paper
before working with your
small group.

3. Reading on Your Own: Partner or Whisper Reading

- Have students take turns reading every other page with a partner or
  have students whisper read on their own.
- Continue having students track each word with their fingers.

4. Comprehension and Skill Work

For students on a 7-Day Plan, tell them that they will do Activity 2 and
work on their Book Journal after they read on their own. Guide practice,
as needed. For teacher directions, see pages 41 and 42. (For 9- to 12-Day
Plans, see the Lesson Planner, page 9.)

5. Homework 2: New Passage

One day Stanley got a letter from his friend Thomas Anthony Jeffrey, whose family had moved recently to California. A school vacation was about to begin, and Stanley was invited to spend it with the Jeffreys.

"Oh, boy!" Stanley said. "I would love to go!"

Mr. Lambchop sighed. "A round-trip train or airplane ticket to California is very expensive," he said. "I will have to think of some cheaper way."

When Mr. Lambchop came home from the office that evening, he brought with him an enormous brown-paper envelope.

"Now then, Stanley," he said. "Try this for size."

The envelope fit Stanley very well. There

16

was even room left over, Mrs. Lambchop discovered, for an egg-salad sandwich made with thin bread, and a toothbrush case filled with milk.

They had to put a great many stamps on the envelope to pay for both airmail and insurance, but it was still much less expensive than a train or airplane ticket to California.

The next day Mr. and Mrs. Lambchop slid Stanley into his envelope, along with the egg-salad sandwich and the toothbrush case full of milk, and mailed him from the box on the corner. The envelope had to be folded to fit through the slot, but Stanley was a limber boy, and inside the box he straightened right up again.

18

Mrs. Lambchop was nervous because Stanley had never been away from home alone before. She rapped on the box.

"Can you hear me, dear?" she called. "Are you all right?"

Stanley's voice came quite clearly. "I'm fine. Can I eat my sandwich now?"

"Wait an hour. And try not to get overheated, dear," Mrs. Lambchop said. Then she and Mr. Lambchop cried out, "Good-bye, good-bye!" and went home.

Stanley had a fine time in California. When the visit was over, the Jeffreys returned him in a beautiful white envelope they had made themselves. It had red-and-blue markings to show that it was airmail, and Thomas Jeffrey had lettered it "Valuable" and

20

"Fragile" and "This End Up" on both sides.

Back home Stanley told his family that he had been handled so carefully he never felt a single bump. Mr. Lambchop said it proved that jet planes were wonderful, and so was the Postal Service, and that this was a great age in which to live.

Stanley thought so too.

21

ENTRY 2

COMPREHENSION PROCESSES

Understand, Apply, Create, Evaluate

WRITING TRAITS

Ideas and Content
Word Choice
Conventions—Complete Sentence,
Capital, Period
Presentation

Responding; Generating Ideas; Using Vocabulary—adventure, round-trip, eventful, fascinating, unique

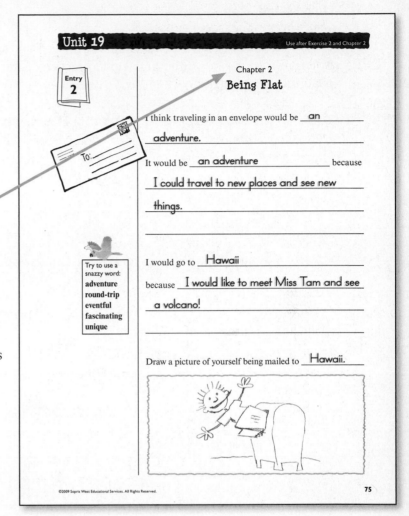

PROCEDURES

For each step, demonstrate and guide practice, as needed. Then have students complete the page independently.

Personal Response: Creative Writing—Specific Instructions

- Have students complete the sentences with creative ideas about what it would be like to travel in an envelope.

- Encourage students to use a snazzy word. Think aloud with students. Say something like:

Find Entry 2 in your Book Journal. Read the first two sentence starters. Use the word *blank* when a word is missing. (I think traveling in an envelope would be blank. It would be blank because . . .)

This is going to be fun. I'm going to look forward to reading your responses.
Read the snazzy words. (adventure, round-trip, eventful, fascinating, unique)
Those would be great words to use in our journals.

I'm going to try using the word *unique*. I might write, "I think traveling in an envelope would be unique." It really would be unique! Now I need to think about why . . .
It would be unique because no one has ever traveled in an envelope.

Hmm . . . I think I'd like to write a little more. It would be unique, but it wouldn't be comfortable!

- As time allows, have students brainstorm other possible answers with the group or with partners.

Self-monitoring

Have students check and correct their work.

STORY COMPREHENSION • MAIN IDEA AND MAZE READING

COMPREHENSION PROCESSES

Understand, Apply

PROCEDURES

For each step, demonstrate and guide practice, as needed. Then have students complete the page independently.

Topic/Main Idea/Supporting Details: Hierarchy Chart—Basic Instructions

- Have students read the main idea sentence and fill in the blank. Say something like:
  Read the sentence in the top box, saying *blank* for the beginning of the sentence.
  (Blank could do many extraordinary things because he was flat.)
  Who is this sentence about? (Stanley)
  Write "Stanley" in the blank, then read the main idea.
  (Stanley could do many extraordinary things because he was flat.)

- Have students fill in three details about things Stanley could do because he was flat.
  Now let's come up with some details from the story that support the main idea.
  What could Stanley do because he was flat?
  (Stanley could slip under doors. Stanley could fly like a kite . . .)

Maze Reading—Basic Instructions

- Have students read the paragraphs and select the word in parentheses that best completes the sentence.
- Have students circle the word, then reread the paragraphs to make sure the whole passage makes sense.

Using Graphic Organizer Identifying— Topic/Who Summarizing— Supporting Details

Comprehension Monitoring, Test Taking

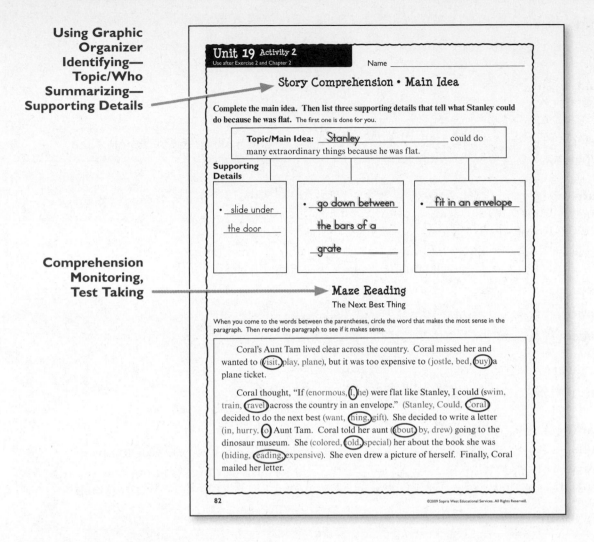

Unit 19 Activity 2
Use after Exercise 2 and Chapter 2

Name _____

Story Comprehension • Main Idea

Complete the main idea. Then list three supporting details that tell what Stanley could do because he was flat. The first one is done for you.

Topic/Main Idea: _Stanley_____ could do many extraordinary things because he was flat.

Supporting Details

- slide under the door

- go down between the bars of a grate

- fit in an envelope

Maze Reading
The Next Best Thing

When you come to the words between the parentheses, circle the word that makes the most sense in the paragraph. Then reread the paragraph to see if it makes sense.

Coral's Aunt Tam lived clear across the country. Coral missed her and wanted to (*visit*, play, plane), but it was too expensive to (jostle, bed, *buy*) a plane ticket.

Coral thought, "If (enormous, *I*, he) were flat like Stanley, I could (swim, train, *travel*) across the country in an envelope." (Stanley, Could, *Coral*) decided to do the next best (want, *thing*, gift). She decided to write a letter (in, hurry, *to*) Aunt Tam. Coral told her aunt (*about*, by, drew) going to the dinosaur museum. She (colored, *told*, special) her about the book she was (hiding, *reading*, expensive). She even drew a picture of herself. Finally, Coral mailed her letter.

©2009 Sopris West Educational Services. All Rights Reserved.

❶ SOUND REVIEW

Use selected Sound Cards from Units 1–19.

❷ SOUND PRACTICE

- For each task, have students spell and say the focus sound in the gray bar. For the Bossy <u>E</u>, read the header.
- Next, have students read each underlined sound, the word, then the whole column.
- Repeat with each column, building accuracy first, then fluency.

> **BUILD ACCURACY AND FLUENCY (Reminder)**
>
> For all rows and columns, follow the specific directions, then build accuracy and fluency with whole words.

❸ ACCURACY AND FLUENCY BUILDING

C1. Multisyllabic Words

- For the list of words divided by syllables, have students read each syllable, then the whole word.
- For the list of whole words, build accuracy and then fluency.

decorate	I drew some pictures to . . . *decorate* . . . my notebook.
college	After high school, some people go to . . . *college.*
opposite	We sat across from one another. We sat . . . *opposite* . . . one another.
trousers	Father wore his white shirt and gray . . . *trousers.*
apologize	When you say you're sorry, you . . . *apologize.*
control	Zippy the dog is big and playful. It's hard to . . . *control* . . . him.
tangling	We tried to fly our kite, but the strink kept . . . *tangling* . . . in the trees.

D1. Tricky Words

- For each Tricky Word, have students use the sounds and word parts they know to silently sound out the word. Use the word in a sentence to help with pronunciation.

roughly

Look at the first word. Say the word parts silently. Thumbs up when you know the word. Use my sentence to help you pronounce the word. The bird pecked the girl when she handled it . . . *roughly.* Read the word three times. (roughly, roughly, roughly)

jostled

Look at the next word. This word is a little tricky, but I think you can figure it out. Sound it out silently, then thumbs up when you're ready. Use my sentence to help you pronounce the word. As Amy walked through the crowd, she got . . . *jostled.* Read the word three times. (jostled, jostled, jostled)

borrowed

Look at the next word. Say the word parts silently. Thumbs up when you know the word. Use my sentence to help you pronounce the word. Lena didn't have a pencil, so she . . . *borrowed* . . . one. Read the word three times. (borrowed, borrowed, borrowed)

patient	The doctor took care of her . . . *patient.*
climbed	Before we slid down the slide, we . . . *climbed* . . . to the top.
eights	Can you count to 16 by . . . *eights?*

- Have students go back and read the whole words in the column.

❹ WORD ENDINGS

❺ MORPHOGRAPHS AND AFFIXES

❻ GENERALIZATION: READING NEW WORDS IN PARAGRAPHS

- Have students read the paragraph silently, then out loud. Tell students to use the sounds and word parts they know to read any difficult words.
- Repeat practice, as needed.

Flat Stanley

Unit 19 Exercise 3
Use before Chapter 3

1. SOUND REVIEW Use selected Sound Cards from Units 1–19.

2. SOUND PRACTICE In each column, have students spell and say the sound, next say any underlined sound and the word, then read the column.

ow as in snow	ph	oo as in moon	ge, -dge	Bossy E
bl<u>ow</u>ing	<u>ph</u>ooey	sp<u>oo</u>l	mana<u>ge</u>	p<u>i</u>led
fl<u>ow</u>n	<u>ph</u>ases	sw<u>oo</u>ped	e<u>dge</u>s	k<u>i</u>tes
rainb<u>ow</u>	Ral<u>ph</u>	l<u>oo</u>p	we<u>dge</u>d	p<u>a</u>le

3. ACCURACY/FLUENCY BUILDING For each column, have students say any underlined part, then read each word. Next, have them read the column.

A1 Mixed Practice	B1 Related Words	C1 Multisyllabic Words		D1 Tricky Words
gusts	roll	dec•o•rate	decorate	roughly
kno<u>ck</u>	rolled	col•lege	college	jostled
for<u>k</u>	unrolled	op•po•site	opposite	borrowed
ta<u>x</u>is	unrolling	trou•sers	trousers	patient
lightly		a•pol•o•gize	apologize	climbed
s<u>oa</u>red		con•trol	control	eights
wind<u>y</u>		tang•ling	tangling	

4. WORD ENDINGS Have students read each underlined word, then the word with an ending.

<u>match</u>ed	<u>hurry</u>ing	<u>speed</u>ing	<u>graceful</u>ly

5. MORPHOGRAPHS AND AFFIXES Have students read the underlined part, then the word.

<u>in</u>crease	accidental<u>ly</u>	<u>un</u>expected	rude<u>ness</u>

6. GENERALIZATION Have students read the paragraph silently, then out loud. (New words: Encyclopaedia Britannica, volumes, parcel)

Arthur had ordered the Encyclopaedia Britannica from a business in California. It was a gift for his mom. An encyclopaedia is a set of books with facts on many subjects. Half the volumes had arrived, but the parcel with the other volumes had not come yet. Arthur was quite worried. He was afraid the parcel had gotten lost. Arthur had been patient, but he finally decided to go the post office to check on the missing volumes.

APPROPRIATE CORRECTIONS
(Reminder)

Write any difficult words on a board or clipboard.

Single-Syllable Pattern Words
Have students identify the difficult sound, then sound out and say the word.

Multisyllabic Words
Draw loops under each word part, then guide practice with your hand.

Tricky Words
Have students sound out or read the word by parts, then say the word. Next have students say, spell, and say the word.

After gently correcting a word with the group, go on to other tasks or words. Return to the difficult word at least three times.

COMPREHENSION PROCESSES

Understand, Apply

PROCEDURES

Introducing Vocabulary

> ★ **jostle** ★ **accidentally** ★ **parcel** ★ **rudeness** ★ **volume, jealous** ★ **manage** ★ **patient**

- For each vocabulary word, have students read the word by parts, then read the whole word.
- Read the student-friendly explanations to students as they follow with their fingers. Then have students use the vocabulary word by following the gray text.
- Review and discuss the illustrations.
  Note: Student vocabulary pages for this unit are found in the students' *Exercise Book 3*.

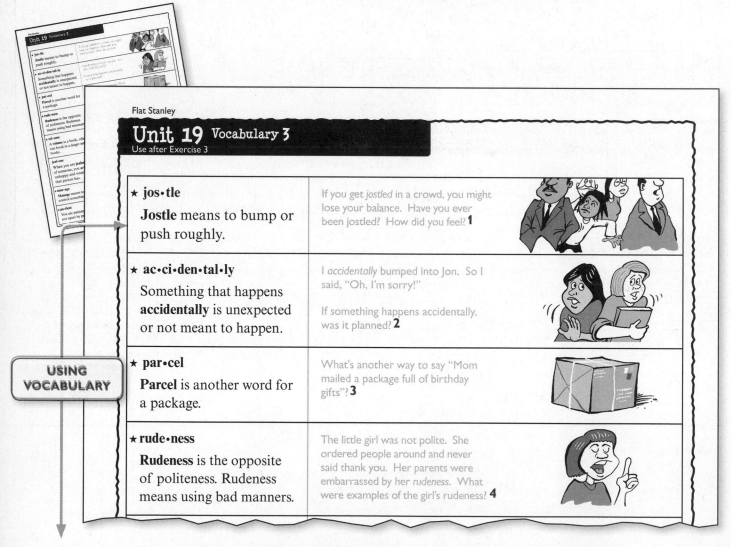

USING VOCABULARY

Flat Stanley

Unit 19 Vocabulary 3
Use after Exercise 3

★ **jos•tle** **Jostle** means to bump or push roughly.	If you get *jostled* in a crowd, you might lose your balance. Have you ever been jostled? How did you feel? **1**	
★ **ac•ci•den•tal•ly** Something that happens **accidentally** is unexpected or not meant to happen.	I *accidentally* bumped into Jon. So I said, "Oh, I'm sorry!" If something happens accidentally, was it planned? **2**	
★ **par•cel** **Parcel** is another word for a package.	What's another way to say "Mom mailed a package full of birthday gifts"? **3**	
★ **rude•ness** **Rudeness** is the opposite of politeness. Rudeness means using bad manners.	The little girl was not polite. She ordered people around and never said thank you. Her parents were embarrassed by her *rudeness*. What were examples of the girl's rudeness? **4**	

❶ **Apply:** Making Connections; Using Vocabulary—jostle (Yes, I have been jostled in a crowd. It made me upset.)

❷ **Understand:** Defining and Using Vocabulary—accidentally (If something happens accidentally, it just happens. It isn't planned.)

❸ **Apply:** Using Vocabulary—parcel (Mom mailed a parcel full of birthday gifts.)

❹ **Understand:** Using Vocabulary—rudeness (The little girl ordered people around and never said thank you.)

★ = New in this unit

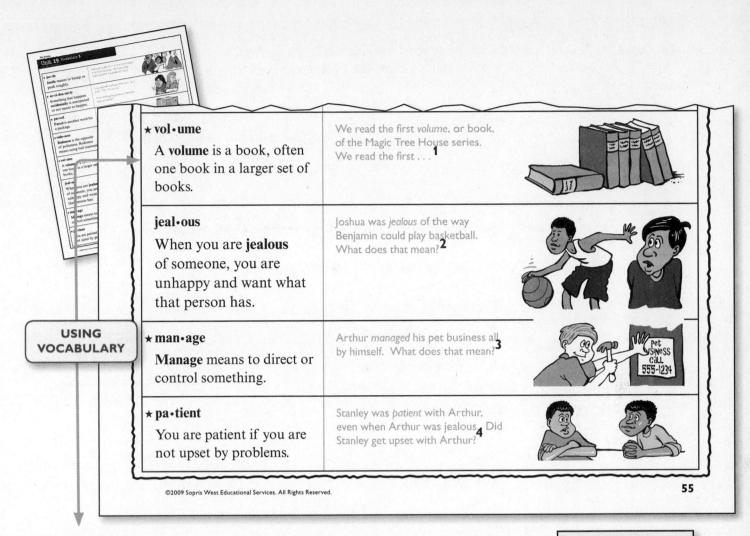

★ vol•ume	We read the first *volume*, or book, of the Magic Tree House series. We read the first . . . **1**	
A **volume** is a book, often one book in a larger set of books.		
jeal•ous	Joshua was *jealous* of the way Benjamin could play basketball. What does that mean? **2**	
When you are **jealous** of someone, you are unhappy and want what that person has.		
★ man•age	Arthur *managed* his pet business all by himself. What does that mean? **3**	
Manage means to direct or control something.		
★ pa•tient	Stanley was *patient* with Arthur, even when Arthur was jealous. Did Stanley get upset with Arthur? **4**	
You are patient if you are not upset by problems.		

55

❶ Apply: Using Vocabulary—volume (volume)

❷ Understand: Defining and Using Vocabulary—jealous (Joshua was unhappy and wished he could play basketball like Benjamin.)

❸ Understand: Defining and Using Vocabulary—manage (Arthur directed and controlled his pet business by himself.)

❹ Understand: Using Vocabulary—patient (No, Stanley was patient and did not get upset.)

USING VOCABULARY

Be enthusiastic about learning new words. Keep a running list of words you would like to use and encourage students to use. Keep the list handy when you are teaching. Put students' names on the board to acknowledge use of a word. Say things like:
Wow! [Heather] used the word *accidentally* when she talked about spilling her juice.

CHAPTER 3 INSTRUCTIONS

Students read pages 22–27 with the teacher and pages 28–33 on their own.
Note: If you're working on a 9- to 12-Day Plan, you will read pages 28–33 with students.

COMPREHENSION PROCESSES

Remember, Understand, Apply, Analyze, Create, Evaluate

PROCEDURES

1. Reviewing Chapters 1 and 2

Summarizing; Identifying—Events, What; Making Connections; Using Vocabulary—absurd, unique

- Quickly review Chapters 1 and 2. Say something like:
  In Chapters 1 and 2, there were several absurd events. What was the first absurd event?
  (A bulletin board fell on Stanley, and he ended up as flat as a pancake.)
  Was Stanley hurt? (no) That's absurd too. It's unbelievable. What else was absurd?
  Would you like to be flat? Why or why not? (Yes, it would be fun and special.)

- Discuss the questions from Chapter 2, Setting a Purpose. Say something like:
  Yesterday, you read pages 16–21 on your own. Let's see what you found out.
  What did Stanley do that was absurd? (He was mailed to California.)
  Why was Mrs. Lambchop nervous? (Stanley had never been away from home.)

  Think aloud.
  That's interesting. If I were Stanley's mom, I would have been worried about his getting bumped around in the mail! I would have worried about him getting sent to the wrong address.

  Why was it awesome to be flat? (Stanley could do all kinds of interesting things. He could travel by mail, go under doors . . .)
  Stanley was one of a kind. He was . . . unique.

2. Introducing Chapter 3

Identifying—Title; Predicting
Discuss Chapter 3. Say something like:
What's the title of this chapter? (Stanley the Kite)
What do you think will happen to Stanley in this chapter? (Stanley will become a kite.)

CORRECTING DECODING ERRORS
During story reading, gently correct any error, then have students reread the sentence.

3. First Reading

- Ask questions and discuss the story as indicated by the blue text in this guide.
- Mix group and individual turns, independent of your voice.
  Have students work toward a group accuracy goal of 0–5 errors.
- After reading the story, practice any difficult words.
  Reread the story if students have not reached the accuracy goal.

4. Second Reading, Short Passage Practice: Developing Prosody

- Demonstrate expressive, fluent reading of the first few paragraphs.
- Guide practice with your voice.
- Provide individual turns while others track with their fingers and whisper read.
- Repeat with one paragraph or page at a time.

Before Reading Page 23

❶ Understand: Viewing, Describing
Look at the picture. Describe what Mr. Lambchop is doing with Stanley.
(He is carrying Stanley, and Stanley is rolled up like a carpet . . .)

❷ Analyze: Drawing Conclusions; **Apply:** Using Vocabulary—jealous
How do you think Arthur feels?
(He looks jealous.)

STANLEY THE KITE

Mr. Lambchop had always liked to take the boys out with him on Sunday afternoons, to a museum or roller-skating in the park, but it was difficult when they were crossing streets or moving about in crowds. Stanley and Arthur would often be jostled from his side and Mr. Lambchop worried about speeding taxis or that hurrying people might

23

COMPREHENSION BUILDING (Reminder)

Encourage students to answer questions with complete sentences. If students have difficulty comprehending, think aloud with them or reread the portion of the story that answers the question. Repeat the question.

accidentally knock them down.

It was easier after Stanley got flat.

Mr. Lambchop discovered that he could roll Stanley up without hurting him at all. He would tie a piece of string around Stanley to keep him from unrolling and make a little loop in the string for himself. It was as simple as carrying a parcel, and he could hold on to Arthur with the other hand.

Stanley did not mind being carried because he had never much liked to walk. Arthur didn't like to walk either, but he had to. It made him mad.

24

One Sunday afternoon, in the street, they met Ralph Jones, an old college friend of Mr. Lambchop's.

"Well, George, I see you have bought some wallpaper," Mr. Jones said. "Going to decorate your house, I suppose?"

"Wallpaper?" said Mr. Lambchop. "Oh, no. This is my son Stanley."

He undid the string and Stanley unrolled.

"How do you do?" Stanley said.

"Nice to meet you, young feller," the man said. "George," he said to Mr. Lambchop, "that boy is flat."

"Smart, too," Mr. Lambchop said. "Stanley is third from the top in his class at school."

"Phooey!" said Arthur.

"This is my younger son, Arthur," Mr.

25

After Reading Pages 24 and 25

❶ Apply: Locating Information, Inferring
In this chapter, Arthur is getting very upset and jealous of Stanley. On pages 24 and 25, there are two places that tell you Arthur is jealous. Look on page 24. Raise your hand when you find the part that tells us Arthur is jealous.
(The books says, "Arthur didn't like to walk either, but he had to. It made him mad.")

❷ Apply: Locating Information, Inferring
Raise your hand when you find the part on page 25 that tells you Arthur is jealous of Stanley.
(The book says, "'Smart too,' Mr. Lampchop said. 'Stanley is third from the top in his class at school.' 'Phooey,' said Arthur.")

❸ Create: Generating Ideas
It sounds like trouble is brewing. What do you think Arthur should do? What do you think Stanley should do?
(Arthur should stop being jealous. Being flat could turn out to be a problem for Stanley. Stanley should try to help his brother get attention . . .)

Lambchop said. "And he will apologize for his rudeness."

Arthur could only blush and apologize.

Mr. Lambchop rolled Stanley up again and they set out for home. It rained quite hard while they were on the way. Stanley, of course, hardly got wet at all, just around the edges, but Arthur got soaked.

Late that night Mr. and Mrs. Lambchop heard a noise out in the living room. They found Arthur lying on the floor near the bookcase. He had piled a great many volumes of the *Encyclopaedia Britannica* on top of himself.

"Put some more on me," Arthur said when he saw them. "Don't just stand there. Help me."

26

After Reading Page 26

❶ Understand: Explaining
What does it mean when the book says, "Arthur could only blush and apologize"?
(Arthur turned red and said he was sorry.)

❷ Apply: Inferring; Explaining; Using Vocabulary—definitely, jealous
What is Arthur doing that tells you he is definitely jealous of Stanley?
(He is trying to get flat so he can be like Stanley.)

CHAPTER 3 INSTRUCTIONS

Students read pages 28–33 without the teacher, independently or
with partners.

Note: If you're working on a 9- to 12-Day Plan, you will read pages 28–33
with students.

COMPREHENSION PROCESSES

Understand

PROCEDURES FOR READING ON YOUR OWN

1. Getting Ready

Have students turn to page 28.

2. Setting a Purpose

Explaining, Inferring

Establish a purpose for reading. Say something like:

Read the next part to find out what Stanley does to help Arthur get over
being jealous. As you read the next pages, try to answer these questions:

- Why did Arthur want to fly a kite?
- Why did Stanley make a good kite?
- What kind of trouble did Stanley get into?
- Why was Stanley mad at Arthur?

> **PREP NOTE**
> **Setting a Purpose**
> Write questions on a
> chalkboard, white board,
> or large piece of paper
> before working with your
> small group.

3. Reading on Your Own: Partner or Whisper Reading

- Have students take turns reading every other page with a partner or
  have students whisper read on their own.
- Continue having students track each word with their fingers.

4. Comprehension and Skill Work

For students on a 7-Day Plan, tell them that they will work on their Book
Journal and do Comprehension and Skill Activity 3 after they read on their
own. Guide practice, as needed. For teacher directions, see pages 56 and
57. (For 9- to 12-Day Plans, see the Lesson Planner, page 9.)

5. Homework 3: New Passage

Mr. and Mrs. Lambchop sent him back to bed, but the next morning they spoke to Stanley. "Arthur can't help being jealous," they said. "Be nice to him. You're his big brother, after all."

The next Sunday, Stanley and Arthur went to the park by themselves. The day was sunny, but windy too, and many older boys were flying beautiful, enormous kites with long tails, made in all the colors of the rainbow.

Arthur sighed. "Someday," he said, "I will have a big kite, and I will win a kite-flying contest and be famous like everyone else. *Nobody* knows who I am these days."

Stanley remembered what his parents had

28

said. He went to a boy whose kite was broken and borrowed a large spool of string.

"You can fly me, Arthur," he said. "Come on."

He attached the string to himself and gave Arthur the spool to hold. He ran lightly across the grass, sideways to get up speed, and then he turned to meet the breeze.

Up, up, up . . . UP! went Stanley, being a kite.

He knew just how to manage on the gusts of wind. He faced full into the wind if he wanted to rise, and let it take him from behind when he wanted speed. He had only to turn his thin edge to the wind, carefully, a little at a time, so that it did not hold him, and then he would slip gracefully down

29

toward the earth again.

Arthur let out all the string, and Stanley soared high above the trees, a beautiful sight in his red shirt and blue trousers, against the pale-blue sky.

Everyone in the park stood still to watch.

Stanley swooped right and then left in long, matched swoops. He held his arms by his sides and zoomed at the ground like a rocket and curved up again toward the sun. He side-slipped and circled, and made figure eights and crosses and a star.

Nobody has ever flown the way Stanley Lambchop flew that day. Probably no one ever will again.

After a while, of course, people grew tired of watching, and Arthur got tired of running

about with the empty spool. Stanley went right on, though, showing off.

Three boys came up to Arthur and invited him to join them for a hot dog and some soda pop. Arthur left the spool wedged in the fork of a tree. He did not notice, while he was eating the hot dog, that the wind was blowing the string and tangling it about the tree.

The string got shorter and shorter, but Stanley did not realize how low he was until leaves brushed his feet, and then it was too late. He got stuck in the branches. Fifteen minutes passed before Arthur and the other boys heard his cries and climbed up to set him free.

Stanley would not speak to his brother that evening, and at bedtime, even though

32

Arthur had apologized, he was still cross.

Alone with Mr. Lambchop in the living room, Mrs. Lambchop sighed and shook her head. "You're at the office all day, having fun," she said. "You don't realize what I go through with the boys. They're very difficult."

"Kids are like that," Mr. Lambchop said. "Phases. Be patient, dear."

33

ENTRY 3

COMPREHENSION PROCESSES

Remember, Understand, Create, Evaluate

WRITING TRAITS

Ideas and Content
Word Choice
Conventions—Complete Sentence, Capital, Period
Presentation

Identifying—How
Using Vocabulary—jealous

Generating Ideas; Using Idioms and
Expressions—bird's-eye view

Responding

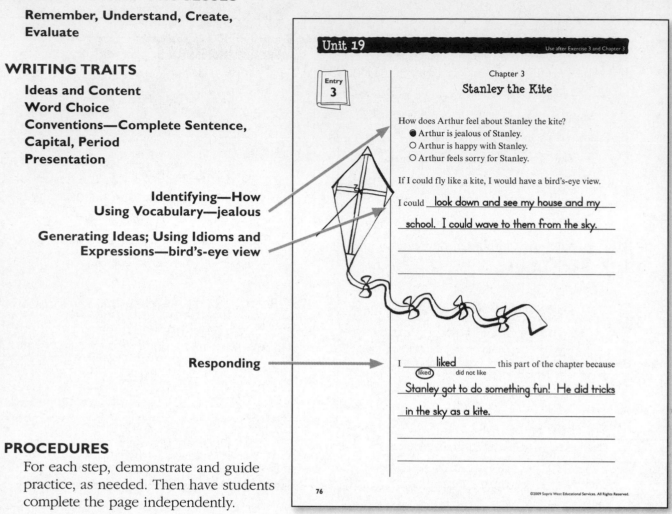

Unit 19   Use after Exercise 3 and Chapter 3

Entry 3

Chapter 3
Stanley the Kite

How does Arthur feel about Stanley the kite?
- ● Arthur is jealous of Stanley.
- ○ Arthur is happy with Stanley.
- ○ Arthur feels sorry for Stanley.

If I could fly like a kite, I would have a bird's-eye view.
I could look down and see my house and my
school. I could wave to them from the sky.

I _____ liked _____ this part of the chapter because
   (liked) / did not like
Stanley got to do something fun! He did tricks
in the sky as a kite.

76   ©2009 Sopris West Educational Services. All Rights Reserved.

PROCEDURES

For each step, demonstrate and guide practice, as needed. Then have students complete the page independently.

1. Selection Response—Basic Instructions

Have students read the question, then fill in the bubble with the answer.

2. Personal Response: Creative Writing—Specific Instructions

Have students complete the sentence starters with their own creative ideas. Encourage students to use snazzy vocabulary words in their writing. Remind them to start sentences with a capital and end with a period. Say something like:

Find Entry 3 in your Book Journal. Read the first sentence.

(If I could fly like a kite, I would have a bird's-eye view.)

What are some things you could do if you could fly like a kite?

(I could see everything below me. I could float in the breeze.)

Remember, we're going to try to use those words in our journals.

Before you write, try to imagine or visualize what it would be like to be a kite. Then think about what you would say.

Self-monitoring

Have students check and correct their work.

VOCABULARY ★ABSURD

COMPREHENSION PROCESSES

Understand

Defining and Using Vocabulary—absurd ⟶

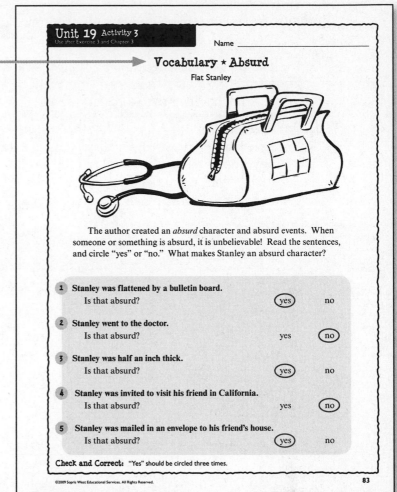

Unit 19 Activity 3
Use after Exercise 3 and Chapter 3

Name _____

Vocabulary ★ Absurd

Flat Stanley

The author created an *absurd* character and absurd events. When someone or something is absurd, it is unbelievable! Read the sentences, and circle "yes" or "no." What makes Stanley an absurd character?

1 **Stanley was flattened by a bulletin board.**
   Is that absurd?   (yes)   no

2 **Stanley went to the doctor.**
   Is that absurd?   yes   (no)

3 **Stanley was half an inch thick.**
   Is that absurd?   (yes)   no

4 **Stanley was invited to visit his friend in California.**
   Is that absurd?   yes   (no)

5 **Stanley was mailed in an envelope to his friend's house.**
   Is that absurd?   (yes)   no

Check and Correct: "Yes" should be circled three times.

83

PROCEDURES

For each step, demonstrate and guide practice, as needed. Then have students complete the page independently.

Vocabulary: Yes/No Selection Response—Specific Instructions
(Items 1–5)

• Have students read the paragraph that defines "absurd." (The author created an absurd character and absurd events . . .)

• Tell students that they will read each sentence, then decide whether the story event is absurd.

• Have students read Item 1. Guide students as they think about the answer. Say something like:
Read Item 1. (Stanley was flattened by a bulletin board.)
Is that an absurd event? (yes)
You're right. If a bulletin board did fall on you, what would happen?
(It would hurt. You might get bruised.)
But you wouldn't become flat. That's absurd. So, what should we circle? (yes)

• Repeat with remaining items, as needed.

Self-monitoring

Have students read the Check and Correct tip. Say something like:
Read the small Check and Correct tip. How many "yes" answers should you have? (three)
What should you do if you have two "yes" answers? (Find one more thing that is absurd.)

★ = New in this unit

❶ SOUND REVIEW

❷ ACCURACY AND FLUENCY BUILDING

B1. Shifty Words

For each word, have students say the underlined sound, sound out the word, and say it.

D1. Buildups

Tell students they can figure out bigger words by building from smaller words.
Have students read the words.

> **BUILD ACCURACY AND FLUENCY**
> **(Reminder)**
> For all rows and columns, follow the specific directions, then build accuracy and fluency with whole words.

E1. Tricky Words

- For each Tricky Word, have students use the sounds and word parts they know to silently sound out the word. Use the word in a sentence to help with pronunciation.
- If the word is unfamiliar, tell students the word.

fierce

Look at the first word. The word is *fierce*. Say the word. (fierce) The growling dog looked . . . *fierce*. Read the word three times. (fierce, fierce, fierce)

suit	Before the party, Leo put on his best . . . *suit*.
signs	When you're driving, it's important to pay attention to the road . . . *signs*.
chief	He is the boss. He's the . . . *chief*.

thief

Look at the next word. This word rhymes with *chief*. Read the word. (thief) Someone who steals is a . . . *thief*. Read the word three times. (thief, thief, thief)

thieves   When there is more than one thief, we say . . . *thieves*.

- Have students go back and read the whole words in the column.

❸ MULTISYLLABIC WORDS

For each word, have students read the syllables, then the whole word. Use the word in a sentence, as appropriate.

suspect	My cookie is gone. I . . . *suspect* . . . my dog ate it.
cleverly	The thief wore a fake wig and disguised himself very . . . *cleverly*.
ringlets	Sheila wore her long, curly hair in . . . *ringlets*.
velvet	The cushions on the couch were made of . . . *velvet*.
meanwhile	I'm going to the park in a little bit. But in the . . . *meanwhile*, . . . I'll do the dishes.
bandanna	The cowboy wore a . . . *bandanna*.

Note: "Bandanna" is spelled with two <u>n</u>'s in this unit but was spelled with one <u>n</u> in Unit 2. Both spellings are acceptable.

❹ WORDS IN CONTEXT

For each word, have students use the sounds and word parts they know to silently sound out the word. Then have students read the sentence. Assist, as needed.

❺ MORPHOGRAPHS AND AFFIXES

- Have students read the underlined part, then the word.
- Repeat practice with whole words, mixing group and individual turns.
  Build accuracy, then fluency.

❻ GENERALIZATION: READING NEW WORDS IN PARAGRAPHS

- Have students read the paragraph silently, then out loud. Tell students to use the sounds and word parts they know to read any difficult words.
- Repeat practice, as needed.

Flat Stanley

Unit 19 Exercise 4
Use before Chapter 4, pages 35-45

1. SOUND REVIEW Have students review sounds for accuracy, then for fluency.

A	-y as in baby	ea as in bread	oo as in book	-dge as in badge	OW as in snow
B	ay	ou	oy	ai	er

2. ACCURACY/FLUENCY BUILDING For each column, have students say any underlined part, then read each word. Next, have them read the column.

A1 Mixed Practice	B1 Shifty Words	C1 Word Endings	D1 Buildups	E1 Tricky Words
fr<u>a</u>me	<u>s</u>ang	shoot<u>ing</u>	sneak	fierce
bl<u>o</u>nd	<u>g</u>ang	ticket<u>s</u>	sneaky	suit
w<u>i</u>fe	<u>h</u>ang	curv<u>ed</u>	sneakery	signs
str<u>aw</u>	hung	guard<u>s</u>		chief
s<u>a</u>sh	sung	ribbon<u>s</u>	gust	thief
flopp<u>y</u>		director<u>s</u>	disgust	thieves
			disgusted	

3. MULTISYLLABIC WORDS Have students read each word part, then the word.

A	sus•pect suspect	clev•er•ly cleverly	ring•lets ringlets
B	vel•vet velvet	mean•while meanwhile	ban•dan•na bandanna

4. WORDS IN CONTEXT For each word, have students use the sounds and word parts they know to figure out the word. Then have them read the sentence.

A	shep•herd•ess	Little Bo Peep is a <u>shepherdess</u>. She takes care of sheep.
B	wits' end	Arthur didn't know what to do. He was at his <u>wits' end</u>.

5. MORPHOGRAPHS AND AFFIXES Have students read the underlined part, then the word.

A	<u>dis</u>like	hope<u>less</u>	permi<u>ssion</u>
B	elevat<u>or</u>	elect<u>ric</u>	ordinari<u>ly</u>

6. GENERALIZATION Have students read the paragraph silently, then out loud. (New words: beard, violin, gloomy, jail)

A man wearing a disguise ran into the Famous Museum of Art. The man wore a wig and a fake beard. He carried a violin. He had just stolen the violin from the music store and was running away from the police.

"They will never find me here," he thought. "I will pretend that I am looking at some paintings."

As he turned the corner, he ran into a policeman, who said, "Caught you! I guess you will be playing some gloomy tunes in jail."

TEACHER: SELF-MONITORING
(Reminder)

- Are you gently correcting all errors?
- Are you returning to difficult words for three correct responses?
- Are you mixing group and individual turns?
- Are you repeating practice until students are accurate and fluent?
- Are you preteaching the lowest performers in your group?

(See *Getting Started* to understand why these strategies are critical to student success.)

COMPREHENSION PROCESSES

Understand, Apply

PROCEDURES

Introducing Vocabulary

★ordinarily ★gloomy ★suspect, permission, disguise ★recognize ★disgusted ★fierce

- For each vocabulary word, have students read the word by parts, then read the whole word.
- Read the student-friendly explanations to students as they follow with their fingers. Then have students use the vocabulary word by following the gray text.
- Review and discuss the illustrations.
  Note: Student vocabulary pages for this unit are found in the students' *Exercise Book 3*.

USING VOCABULARY

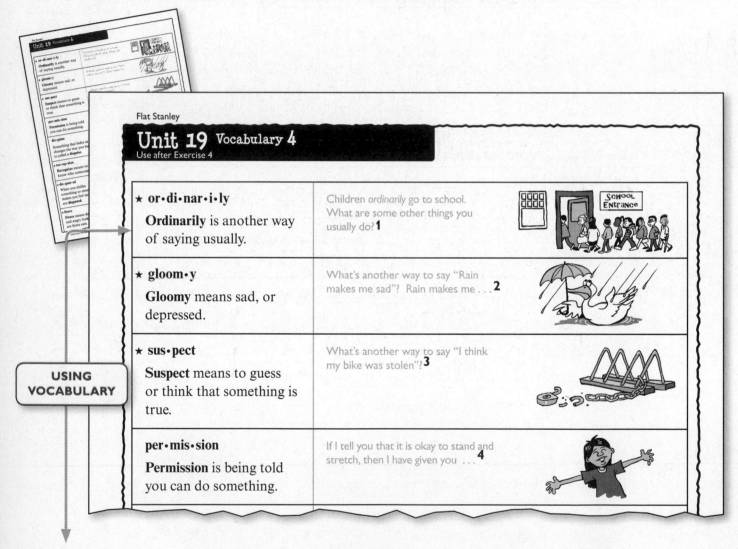

Flat Stanley

Unit 19 Vocabulary 4
Use after Exercise 4

★ or•di•nar•i•ly **Ordinarily** is another way of saying usually.	Children *ordinarily* go to school. What are some other things you usually do? **1**
★ gloom•y **Gloomy** means sad, or depressed.	What's another way to say "Rain makes me sad"? Rain makes me . . . **2**
★ sus•pect **Suspect** means to guess or think that something is true.	What's another way to say "I think my bike was stolen"? **3**
per•mis•sion **Permission** is being told you can do something.	If I tell you that it is okay to stand and stretch, then I have given you . . . **4**

❶ **Apply:** Making Connections; Using Vocabulary—ordinarily (I ordinarily brush my teeth at night.)

❷ **Apply:** Using Vocabulary—gloomy (gloomy)

❸ **Apply:** Using Vocabulary—suspect (I suspect my bike was stolen.)

❹ **Understand:** Using Vocabulary—permission (permission)

★ = New in this unit

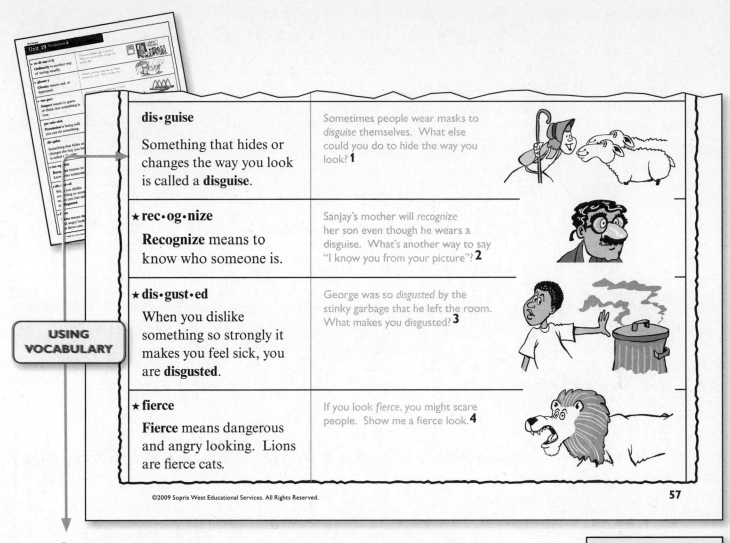

USING VOCABULARY

dis•guise Something that hides or changes the way you look is called a **disguise**.	Sometimes people wear masks to *disguise* themselves. What else could you do to hide the way you look? **1**	
★ **rec•og•nize** **Recognize** means to know who someone is.	Sanjay's mother will *recognize* her son even though he wears a disguise. What's another way to say "I know you from your picture"? **2**	
★ **dis•gust•ed** When you dislike something so strongly it makes you feel sick, you are **disgusted**.	George was so *disgusted* by the stinky garbage that he left the room. What makes you disgusted? **3**	
★ **fierce** **Fierce** means dangerous and angry looking. Lions are fierce cats.	If you look *fierce*, you might scare people. Show me a fierce look. **4**	

57

❶ **Apply:** Using Vocabulary—disguise (You could wear a wig to disguise yourself.)

❷ **Apply:** Using Vocabulary—recognize (I recognize you from your picture.)

❸ **Apply:** Making Connections; Using Vocabulary—disgusted (I am disgusted by the smell of gasoline . . .)

❹ **Apply:** Demonstrating; Using Vocabulary—fierce

USING VOCABULARY

Be enthusiastic about learning new words. Keep a running list of words you would like to use and encourage students to use. Keep the list handy when you are teaching. Put students' names on the board to acknowledge use of a word. Say things like:

Wow! [Myschell] used the word *permission* when she asked if she could go to the bathroom.

STORY READING INSTRUCTIONS
Students read pages 34–39 with the teacher and pages 39–45 on their own. Page 39 is split between reading sections.

COMPREHENSION PROCESSES
Remember, Understand, Apply

PROCEDURES

1. Reviewing Chapter 3

Summarizing; Inferring; Using Vocabulary—jealous, brag

- Discuss Chapter 3. Say something like:

   In Chapter 3, we found out that Arthur was very jealous of Stanley. How could we tell?

   (Arthur tried to get flat by putting books on his chest. He said "Phooey" when Mr. Lambchop bragged about Stanley.)

   What did Stanley do to help Arthur feel better?

   (Stanley let Arthur fly him like a kite.)

> **PREP NOTE**
> Students will stop and start reading in the middle of pages 39, 49, and 60. Mark those places in students' books with a sticky strip.

- Discuss the questions from Chapter 3, Setting a Purpose. Say something like:

   Yesterday, you read pages 28–33 on your own. Let's see what you found out.

   Why did Arthur want to fly a kite? (He thought people would pay attention to him.)

   Why did Stanley make a good kite?

   (He knew how to go up and down and swoop from side to side . . .)

   What kind of trouble did Stanley get into? (He got stuck in a tree.)

   Why was Stanley mad at Arthur? (Arthur forgot about Stanley and left him in the tree.)

2. Introducing Chapter 4

Defining, Predicting

Discuss Chapter 3. Say something like:

This chapter is called "The Museum Thieves." What are thieves? (Thieves are people who steal.)

What do you think is going to happen in this chapter?

(Someone will steal something from the museum . . .)

3. First Reading

- Ask questions and discuss the story as indicated by the blue text in this guide.
- Mix group and individual turns, independent of your voice.
   Have students work toward a group accuracy goal of 0–5 errors.
   Quietly keep track of errors made by all students in the group.
- After reading the story, practice any difficult words.
   Reread the story if students have not reached the accuracy goal.

4. Second Reading, Timed Readings: Repeated Reading

- As time allows, have students do Timed Readings while others follow along.
- Time individuals for 30 seconds and encourage each child to work for a personal best.
- Determine words correct per minute. Record student scores.

THE MUSEUM THIEVES

Mr. and Mrs. O. Jay Dart lived in the apartment above the Lambchops. Mr. Dart was an important man, the director of the Famous Museum of Art downtown in the city.

Stanley Lambchop had noticed in the elevator that Mr. Dart, who was ordinarily a cheerful man, had become quite gloomy, but he had no idea what the reason was.

35

After Reading Page 35

❶ **Remember:** Identifying—Who
Who is Mr. Dart?
(Mr. Dart is the Lambchops' neighbor and the director of the museum.)

❷ **Understand:** Viewing, Describing
You can tell by the picture Mr. Dart is very unhappy. What is he doing in the picture?
(He is leaning his head against the wall.)

❸ **Apply:** Inferring—Problem; Explaining
Stanley doesn't know what the problem is. What is Mr. Dart's problem? How can you tell?
(His museum was robbed . . . The title of the chapter is "The Museum Thieves.")

And then at breakfast one morning he heard Mr. and Mrs. Lambchop talking about Mr. Dart.

"I see," said Mr. Lambchop, reading the paper over his coffee cup, "that still another painting has been stolen from the Famous Museum. It says here that Mr. O. Jay Dart, the director, is at his wits' end."

"Oh, dear! Are the police no help?" Mrs. Lambchop asked.

"It seems not," said Mr. Lambchop. "Listen to what the Chief of Police told the newspaper. 'We suspect a gang of sneak thieves. These are the worst kind. They work by sneakery, which makes them very difficult to catch. However, my men and I will keep trying. Meanwhile, I hope people will buy

36

After Reading Page 36

❶ **Apply:** Inferring, Explaining
The book says that Mr. Dart was at his wits' end. What do you think that means?
(He didn't know what else to do. He was upset . . .)

❷ **Remember:** Identifying—Who
Who do the police think are stealing the paintings?
(The police think sneak thieves are stealing the paintings.)

tickets for the Policemen's Ball and not park their cars where signs say don't.' "

The next morning Stanley Lambchop heard Mr. Dart talking to his wife in the elevator.

"These sneak thieves work at night," Mr. Dart said. "It is very hard for our guards to stay awake when they have been on duty all day. And the Famous Museum is so big, we cannot guard every picture at the same time. I fear it is hopeless, hopeless, hopeless!"

Suddenly, as if an electric light bulb had lit up in the air above his head, giving out little shooting lines of excitement, Stanley Lambchop had an idea. He told it to Mr. Dart.

"Stanley," Mr. Dart said, "if your mother will give her permission, I will put you and

38

your plan to work this very night!"

Mrs. Lambchop gave her permission. "But you will have to take a long nap this afternoon," she said. "I won't have you up till all hours unless you do."

That evening, after a long nap, Stanley went with Mr. Dart to the Famous Museum. Mr. Dart took him into the main hall, where

39

Stop Reading Here ←

After Reading Page 39 (top half)

❶ **Apply:** Inferring, Explaining
Mr. Dart said, "I fear it is hopeless." What did he mean?
(They wouldn't catch the thieves. The thieves would keep stealing paintings.)

❷ **Apply:** Inferring, Explaining
Why does Mr. Dart think they won't catch the thieves?
(The thieves work at night. The guards can't stay awake. The museum is too big to guard every picture.)

❸ **Apply:** Predicting
Stanley has a plan. What do you think he is going to do?

STORY READING INSTRUCTIONS

Students read pages 39–45 without the teacher, independently or with partners. Page 39 is split between reading sections.

COMPREHENSION PROCESSES

Remember, Understand

PROCEDURES

1. Getting Ready

Have students turn to page 39.

2. Setting a Purpose

Defining and Using Vocabulary—disguise; Identifying—What, Where; Explaining

Before you begin reading, say something like:

Next, you are going to find out about Stanley's plan to catch the thieves. It involves a disguise. What is a disguise?

(A disguise is something that changes the way you look.)

As you read the next pages, try to answer these questions:
- What disguise did Stanley want to wear?
- What disguise did Mr. Dart have for Stanley?
- Why did Mr. Dart pick that disguise for Stanley?
- Where did Stanley hide?

3. Reading on Your Own: Partner or Whisper Reading

- Have students take turns reading every other page with a partner or have students whisper read pages 39–45 on their own. Say something like:

  Everyone, put your finger on the last paragraph on page 39. It starts, "That evening . . . "

  This is where you're going to start reading on your own—without me.

  Now turn to page 44. You will stop reading at the bottom of the page.

- Continue having students track each word with their fingers.

4. Comprehension and Skill Work

For students on a 7-Day Plan, tell them that they will work on their Book Journal and do Comprehension and Skill Activity 4 after they read on their own. Guide practice, as needed. For teacher directions, see pages 71 and 72. (For 9- to 12-Day Plans, see the Lesson Planner, page 9.)

5. Homework 4: New Passage

your plan to work this very night!"

Mrs. Lambchop gave her permission. "But you will have to take a long nap this afternoon," she said. "I won't have you up till all hours unless you do."

Start Reading Here →

That evening, after a long nap, Stanley went with Mr. Dart to the Famous Museum. Mr. Dart took him into the main hall, where

39

the biggest and most important paintings were hung. He pointed to a huge painting that showed a bearded man, wearing a floppy velvet hat, playing a violin for a lady who lay on a couch. There was a half-man, half-horse person standing behind them, and three fat children with wings were flying around above. That, Mr. Dart explained, was the most expensive painting in the world!

There was an empty picture frame on the opposite wall. We shall hear more about that later on.

Mr. Dart took Stanley into his office and said, "It is time for you to put on a disguise."

"I already thought of that," Stanley Lambchop said, "and I brought one. My cowboy suit. It has a red bandanna that I can tie

40

over my face. Nobody will recognize me in a million years."

"No," Mr. Dart said. "You will have to wear the disguise I have chosen."

From a closet he took a white dress with a blue sash, a pair of shiny little pointed shoes, a wide straw hat with a blue band that matched the sash, and a wig and a stick. The wig was made of blond hair, long and done in ringlets. The stick was curved at the top and it, too, had a blue ribbon on it.

"In this shepherdess disguise," Mr. Dart said, "you will look like a painting that belongs in the main hall. We do not have cowboy pictures in the main hall."

Stanley was so disgusted, he could hardly speak. "I will look like a girl, that's what I will

42

look like," he said. "I wish I had never had my idea."

But he was a good sport, so he put on the disguise.

Back in the main hall, Mr. Dart helped Stanley climb up into the empty picture frame. Stanley was able to stay in place because Mr. Dart had cleverly put four small spikes in the wall, one for each hand and foot.

The frame was a perfect fit. Against the wall, Stanley looked just like a picture.

"Except for one thing," Mr. Dart said. "Shepherdesses are supposed to look happy. They smile at their sheep and at the sky. You look fierce, not happy, Stanley."

Stanley tried hard to get a faraway look in his eyes and even to smile a little bit.

44

ENTRY 4

COMPREHENSION PROCESSES

Understand, Create, Apply, Evaluate

WRITING TRAITS

Ideas and Content
Word Choice
Conventions—Complete Sentence,
Capital, Period
Presentation

Responding; Generating Ideas; Sentence Completion; Illustrating; Using Vocabulary—recognize, sensational

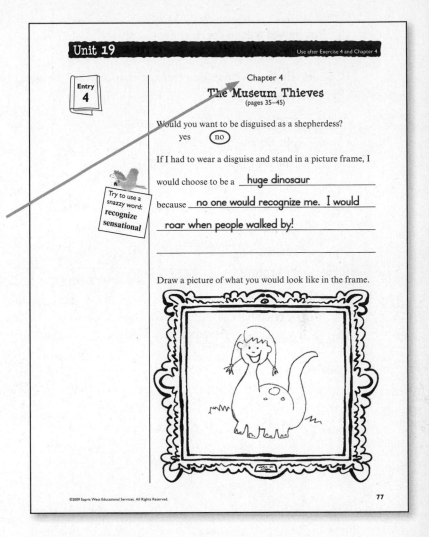

Unit 19
Use after Exercise 4 and Chapter 4

Entry 4

Chapter 4
The Museum Thieves
(pages 35–45)

Would you want to be disguised as a shepherdess?

yes   (no)

If I had to wear a disguise and stand in a picture frame, I would choose to be a huge dinosaur

because no one would recognize me. I would roar when people walked by!

Try to use a snazzy word:
recognize
sensational

Draw a picture of what you would look like in the frame.

©2009 Sopris West Educational Services. All Rights Reserved.

77

PROCEDURES

For each step, demonstrate and guide practice, as needed. Then have students complete the page independently.

Personal Response: Creative Writing, Illustrating—Specific Instructions
- Have students answer the first question by circling "yes" or "no."
- Have students complete the sentence starters with their own creative ideas. Encourage students to use snazzy vocabulary words in their writing. Remind them to start sentences with a capital and end with a period.
- Have students illustrate their ideas.

Self-monitoring

Have students check and correct their work.

STORY COMPREHENSION

COMPREHENSION PROCESSES

Remember, Understand, Apply

WRITING TRAITS

Conventions—Complete Sentence, Capital, Period
Presentation

PROCEDURES

For each step, demonstrate and guide practice, as needed. Then have students complete the page independently.

1. **Selection Response: Sentence Writing—Basic Instructions** (Item 1, 3)
   Have students read the sentence starter or question, then fill in the bubble and/or blank with the correct answer. Remind them to use a capital and period.

2. **Sentence Writing—Basic Instructions** (Item 2)
   Have students read the question and write a complete sentence answer. Tell them to start their sentence with what the question is about. The words are underlined. Remind students to start sentences with a capital and end with a period.

Self-monitoring
Have students check and correct their work.

**Explaining—
Character Traits
(Characterization)**

**Inferring
Explaining—
Character Traits
(Characterization)**

Identifying—Action

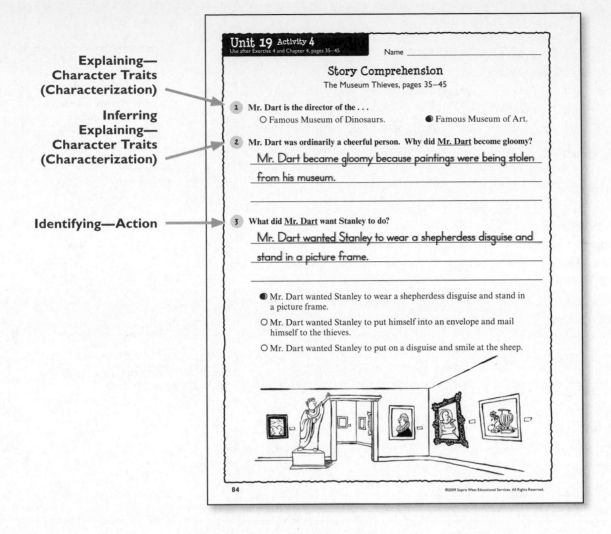

Unit 19 Activity 4
Use after Exercise 4 and Chapter 4, pages 35—45

Name _____

Story Comprehension
The Museum Thieves, pages 35—45

1. Mr. Dart is the director of the . . .
   ○ Famous Museum of Dinosaurs.   ● Famous Museum of Art.

2. Mr. Dart was ordinarily a cheerful person. Why did <u>Mr. Dart</u> become gloomy?

   <u>Mr. Dart became gloomy because paintings were being stolen</u>

   <u>from his museum.</u>

3. What did <u>Mr. Dart</u> want Stanley to do?

   <u>Mr. Dart wanted Stanley to wear a shepherdess disguise and</u>

   <u>stand in a picture frame.</u>

   ● Mr. Dart wanted Stanley to wear a shepherdess disguise and stand in
     a picture frame.
   ○ Mr. Dart wanted Stanley to put himself into an envelope and mail
     himself to the thieves.
   ○ Mr. Dart wanted Stanley to put on a disguise and smile at the sheep.

84   ©2009 Sopris West Educational Services. All Rights Reserved.

❶ SOUND REVIEW

❷ ACCURACY AND FLUENCY BUILDING

C1. Multisyllabic Words

- For the list of words divided by syllables, have students read each syllable, then the whole word.
- For the list of whole words, build accuracy and then fluency.

civilized	When you behave in a polite way, you are acting . . . *civilized.*
opposite	The picture is on the wall across the room. It is on the . . . *opposite* . . . wall.
disgusted	When the cat got sick in the car, Jong was . . . *disgusted.*
crazy	When the fireworks start, my dog barks and goes . . . *crazy.*
prickle	Alani touched the thorny plant and felt a . . . *prickle.*
trapdoor	We enter our secret hideout through a . . . *trapdoor.*
secret	Something that is hidden or that you don't tell is a . . . *secret.*
moonlight	When the moon is full, we can see by the . . . *moonlight.*

D1. Tricky Words

- For each Tricky Word, have students use the sounds and word parts they know to silently sound out the word. Use the word in a sentence to help with pronunciation.

answer	Please give me your . . . *answer.*
chief	The head of the police department is the . . . *chief.*
certain	Let's check the amount again, so we'll be . . . *certain* . . . it is correct.
especially	I like apples . . . *especially* . . . red ones.
thieves	People who steal are called . . . *thieves.*

- Have students go back and read the whole words in the column.

❸ WORD ENDINGS

❹ WORDS IN CONTEXT

For each word, have students use the sounds and word parts they know to silently sound out the word. Then have students read the sentence. Assist, as needed.

❺ MORPHOGRAPHS AND AFFIXES

- Remind students that a morphograph is a word part that has meaning.
- ★Introduce "im = not."
  Look at Row A. The morphograph *im-* means not. So we can say that *im-* equals not.
  Everyone, read that with me. *Im- equals not.*
- For each word, have students read what the word means and the accompanying sentence. Have students rephrase the sentence.
  Im- means not, so *impossible* means not possible. Read the sentence.
  (A tall tale is impossible.) That means a tall tale is . . . *not possible.*
- Repeat with "impure equals not pure."
- For Row C, have students read the underlined part, then the word.

★ = New in this unit

❻ GENERALIZATION: READING NEW WORDS IN PARAGRAPHS

- Have students read the paragraph silently, then out loud. Tell students to use the sounds and word parts they know to read any difficult words.
- Repeat practice, as needed.

Flat Stanley

Unit 19 Exercise 5
Use before Chapter 4, pages 46-54

1. SOUND REVIEW Use select Sound Cards from Units 1–19.

2. ACCURACY/FLUENCY BUILDING For each column, have students say any underlined part, then read each word. Next, have them read the column.

A1 Mixed Practice	**B1** Rhyming Words	**C1** Multisyllabic Words		**D1** Tricky Words
c<u>au</u>ses	picture	civ•i•lized	civilized	answer
c<u>ur</u>ls	capture	op•po•site	opposite	chief
joke		dis•gust•ed	disgusted	certain
cr<u>ea</u>k	hey	cra•zy	crazy	especially
v<u>oi</u>ce	obey	prick•le	prickle	thieves
polite	curious	trap•door	trapdoor	
pi<u>tch</u>	furious	se•cret	secret	
		moon•light	moonlight	

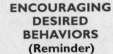

3. WORD ENDINGS Have students read each word set.

balance	balancing	manage	managed	reply	replied

4. WORDS IN CONTEXT Have students use the sounds and word parts they know to figure out each word. Then have them read each sentence.

Ⓐ	sen•sa•tion•al	The show was really great. It was <u>sensational</u>.
Ⓑ	e•mo•tion	An <u>emotion</u> is how you feel. An emotion can be glad, sad, or mad.
Ⓒ	whilst	Dan ate <u>whilst</u> he worked. This is an old way of saying *while*.

5. MORPHOGRAPHS AND AFFIXES Have students practice reading "im = not" and the related words and sentences. For Row C, have students read the underlined part, then the word.

Ⓐ	★im = not	impossible = not possible	A tall tale is <u>impossible</u>.
Ⓑ		impure = not pure	The water was <u>impure</u>.
Ⓒ	<u>be</u>neath	<u>medal</u>	dark<u>ness</u>	absolute<u>ly</u>

6. GENERALIZATION Have students read the paragraph silently, then out loud. (New words: arrested, handcuffed, terrifying, quivery)

Luther and his brother, Max, were waiting at the entrance to the world famous magic show when they suddenly heard a huge commotion. They turned and saw that policemen had arrested and handcuffed some bearded robbers. The terrifying event left the brothers feeling quivery inside. The Chief of Police told everyone to be calm. Then the police took the thieves to jail.

COMPREHENSION PROCESSES

Apply

PROCEDURES

Introducing Vocabulary

| ☆entrance ☆sensational ☆civilized, suspect ☆reply ☆furious |

- For each vocabulary word, have students read the word by parts, then read the whole word.
- Read the student-friendly explanations to students as they follow with their fingers. Then have students use the vocabulary word by following the gray text.
- Review and discuss the illustrations.

  Note: Student vocabulary pages for this unit are found in the students' *Exercise Book 3*.

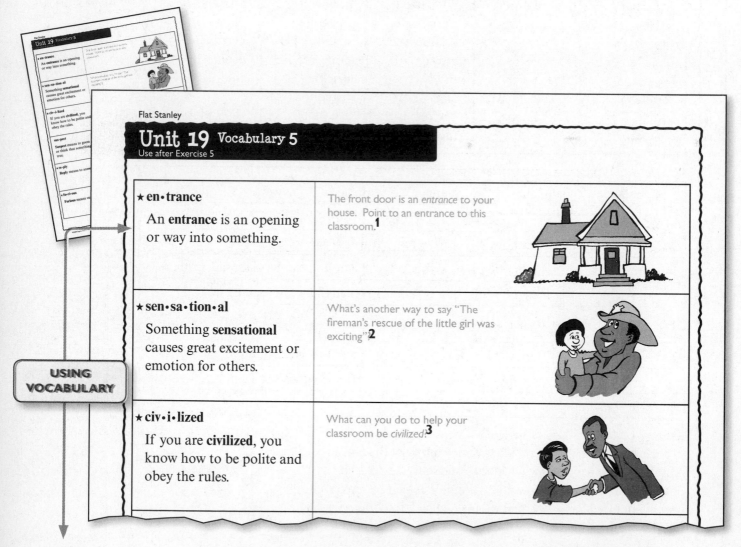

USING VOCABULARY

Flat Stanley

Unit 19 Vocabulary 5
Use after Exercise 5

★ en•trance An **entrance** is an opening or way into something.	The front door is an *entrance* to your house. Point to an entrance to this classroom.**1**	
★ sen•sa•tion•al Something **sensational** causes great excitement or emotion for others.	What's another way to say "The fireman's rescue of the little girl was exciting"?**2**	
★ civ•i•lized If you are **civilized**, you know how to be polite and obey the rules.	What can you do to help your classroom be *civilized*?**3**	

❶ **Apply:** Demonstrating; Using Vocabulary—entrance

❷ **Apply:** Using Vocabulary—sensational (The fireman's rescue of the little girl was sensational.)

❸ **Apply:** Making Connections; Using Vocabulary—civilized (I can be polite and obey the rules to help our classroom be civilized.)

☆ = New in this unit

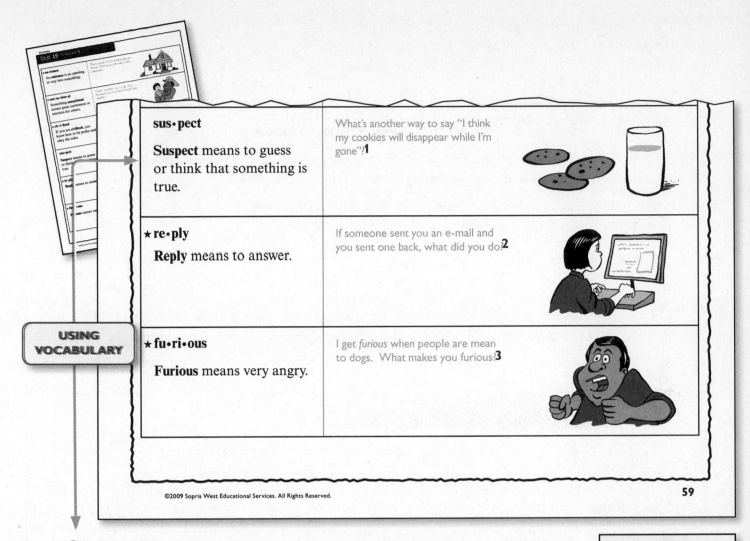

USING VOCABULARY

sus•pect **Suspect** means to guess or think that something is true.	What's another way to say "I think my cookies will disappear while I'm gone"?**1**	
★ **re•ply** **Reply** means to answer.	If someone sent you an e-mail and you sent one back, what did you do?**2**	
★ **fu•ri•ous** **Furious** means very angry.	I get *furious* when people are mean to dogs. What makes you furious?**3**	

59

❶ **Apply:** Using Vocabulary—suspect (I suspect my cookies will disappear while I'm gone.)

❷ **Apply:** Using Vocabulary—reply (I replied to the e-mail.)

❸ **Apply:** Making Connections; Using Vocabulary—furious (I get furious when people call me names.)

USING VOCABULARY

Be enthusiastic about learning new words. Keep a running list of words you would like to use and encourage students to use. Keep the list handy when you are teaching. Put students' names on the board to acknowledge use of a word. Say things like:

[Mary] used the word *sensational* when she talked about the book she was reading. What a great way to use a vocabulary word!

STORY READING INSTRUCTIONS

Students read pages 46–49 with the teacher and pages 49–53 on their own. Page 49 is split between reading sections.

COMPREHENSION PROCESSES

Remember, Understand, Apply

PROCEDURES

1. **Reviewing Chapter 4, pages 35–45**

   Summarizing; Explaining—Problem, Solution; Identifying—What, Where; Using Vocabulary—disguise; Making Connections

   - Have students quickly review what has happened so far in Chapter 4. Say something like:

     In the first part of Chapter 4, what was Mr. Dart's problem?
     (Thieves were stealing paintings from his museum.)

     What was Stanley's plan to catch the thieves? (Stanley's plan was to disguise himself as a painting and catch the thieves in the act.)

   - Discuss the questions from the previous Setting a Purpose.
     Yesterday, you read pages 39–45 on your own. Let's see what you found out.
     What disguise did Stanley want to wear?
     (He wanted to wear a cowboy disguise.)
     What disguise did Mr. Dart have for Stanley?
     (Mr. Dart had a shepherdess disguise for Stanley.)
     Why did Mr. Dart pick that disguise for Stanley? (Stanley needed to look like a painting in the main hall. There were no cowboy paintings in the main hall.)
     Where did Stanley hide? (Stanley hid in a frame on the wall near the most expensive painting in the world.)

     If you had to wear a disguise, what would you have chosen?
     (a ballerina, a show dog . . .)

   > **PREP NOTE**
   > Students will stop and start reading in the middle of pages 39, 49, and 60. Mark those places in students' books with a sticker, an arrow, or sticky note.

   > **CORRECTING DECODING ERRORS**
   > During story reading, gently correct any error, then have students reread the sentence.

2. **Introducing Chapter 4, pages 46–49**

   Predicting

   Have students predict what they think will happen next.

3. **First Reading**
   - Ask questions and discuss the story as indicated by the blue text in this guide.
   - Mix group and individual turns, independent of your voice.
     Have students work toward a group accuracy goal of 0–5 errors.
   - After reading the story, practice any difficult words.
     Repeat if students have not reached the accuracy goal.

4. **Second Reading, Short Passage Practice: Developing Prosody**
   - Demonstrate expressive, fluent reading on the first paragraph. Read at a rate slightly faster than the students' rate.
   - Guide practice with your voice.
   - Provide individual turns while others track with their fingers and whisper read.
   - Repeat with one paragraph or one page at a time.

Mr. Dart stood back a few feet and stared at him for a moment. "Well," he said, "it may not be art, but I know what I like."

He went off to make sure that certain other parts of Stanley's plan were taken care of, and Stanley was left alone.

It was very dark in the main hall. A little bit of moonlight came through the windows, and Stanley could just make out the world's most expensive painting on the opposite wall. He felt as though the bearded man with the violin and the lady on the couch and the half-horse person and the winged children were all waiting, as he was, for something to happen.

Time passed and he got tireder and tireder. Anyone would be tired this late at night,

46

especially if he had to stand in a picture frame balancing on little spikes.

Maybe they won't come, Stanley thought. Maybe the sneak thieves won't come at all.

The moon went behind a cloud and then the main hall was pitch-dark. It seemed to get quieter, too, with the darkness. There was absolutely no sound at all. Stanley felt the hair on the back of his neck prickle beneath the golden curls of the wig.

Cr-eee-eee-k . . .

The creaking sound came from right out in the middle of the main hall, and even as he heard it, Stanley saw, in the same place, a tiny yellow glow of light!

The creaking came again, and the glow got bigger. A trapdoor had opened in the

47

After Reading Page 46

❶ **Understand:** Identifying—Where
Where is Stanley standing?
(He is standing in a picture.)

After Reading Page 47

❶ **Apply:** Predicting
What do you think is going to happen next?
(The robbers are going to come up through the trapdoor.)

floor, and two men came up through it into the hall!

Stanley understood everything all at once. These must be the sneak thieves! They had a secret trap door entrance into the museum from outside. That was why they had never been caught. And now, tonight, they were back to steal the most expensive painting in the world!

He held very still in his picture frame and listened to the sneak thieves.

"This is it, Max," said the first one. "This is where we art robbers pull a sensational job whilst the civilized community sleeps."

Stop Reading Here

"Right, Luther," said the other man. "In all this great city, there is no one to suspect us."

Ha, ha! thought Stanley Lambchop. That's what you think!

The sneak thieves put down their lantern and took the world's most expensive painting off the wall.

"What would we do to anyone who tried to

49

After Reading Page 49 (top half)

❶ **Understand:** Explaining
Why hadn't the thieves been caught?
(They were getting into and out of the museum through a trapdoor.)

STORY READING INSTRUCTIONS

Students read pages 49–53 without the teacher, independently or with partners. Page 49 is split between reading sections.

Note: If you're working on a 9- to 12-Day plan, you will read pages 49–53 with students.

COMPREHENSION PROCESSES

Understand

PROCEDURES

1. Getting Ready

Have students turn to page 49.

2. Setting a Purpose

Explaining—What, Events, End/Conclusion

Before you begin reading, say something like:

Read the last part of the chapter to find out why Stanley became frightened and the outcome of his plan. Read to find out the answers to these questions.

- What would the thieves do to anyone who tried to capture them?
- Why did Stanley yell? What did he yell?
- What happened to the thieves?
- What happened at the end of the chapter?

> **PREP NOTE**
> **Setting a Purpose**
> Write questions on a chalkboard, white board, or large piece of paper before working with your small group.

3. Reading on Your Own: Partner or Whisper Reading

- Have students take turns reading every other page with a partner or have students whisper read pages 49–53 on their own.

  Everyone, look at page 49. Find the paragraph in the middle of the page where it says, "Right, Luther."

  This is where you will start reading on your own—without me.

  Now turn to page 53. That's the last page in the chapter. Stop there.

- Continue having students track each word with their fingers.

4. Comprehension and Skill Work

For students on a 7-Day Plan, tell them that they will do Activity 5 and work on their Book Journal after they read on their own. Guide practice, as needed. For teacher directions, see pages 85 and 86. (For 9- to 12-Day Plans, see the Lesson Planner, page 9.)

5. Homework 5: New Passage

Start Reading Here

they had never been caught. And now, tonight, they were back to steal the most expensive painting in the world!

He held very still in his picture frame and listened to the sneak thieves.

"This is it, Max," said the first one. "This is where we art robbers pull a sensational job whilst the civilized community sleeps."

"Right, Luther," said the other man. "In all this great city, there is no one to suspect us."

Ha, ha! thought Stanley Lambchop. That's what you think!

The sneak thieves put down their lantern and took the world's most expensive painting off the wall.

"What would we do to anyone who tried to

49

capture us, Max?" the first man asked.

"We would kill him. What else?" his friend replied.

That was enough to frighten Stanley, and he was even more frightened when Luther came over and stared at him.

"This sheep girl," Luther said. "I thought sheep girls were supposed to smile, Max. This one looks scared."

Just in time, Stanley managed to get a faraway look in his eyes again and to smile, sort of.

"You're crazy, Luther," Max said. "She's smiling. And what a pretty little thing she is, too."

That made Stanley furious. He waited until the sneak thieves had turned back to

50

the world's most expensive painting, and he shouted in his loudest, most terrifying voice: "POLICE! POLICE! MR. DART! THE SNEAK THIEVES ARE HERE!"

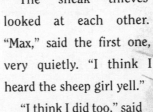

The sneak thieves looked at each other. "Max," said the first one, very quietly. "I think I heard the sheep girl yell."

"I think I did too," said Max in a quivery voice. "Oh, boy! Yelling pictures. We both need a rest."

"You'll get a rest, all right!" shouted Mr. Dart, rushing in with the Chief of Police and lots of guards and policemen behind him. "You'll get *ar-rested*, that's what! Ha, ha, ha!"

The sneak thieves were too mixed up by

Mr. Dart's joke and too frightened by the policemen to put up a fight.

Before they knew it, they had been hand-cuffed and led away to jail.

The next morning in the office of the Chief of Police, Stanley Lambchop got a medal. The day after that his picture was in all the newspapers.

ENTRY 5

COMPREHENSION PROCESSES

Understand, Evaluate

WRITING TRAITS

Ideas and Content
Conventions—Complete Sentence,
Capital, Period
Presentation

Responding; Sentence Completion
Using Vocabulary—
impressed; Explaining

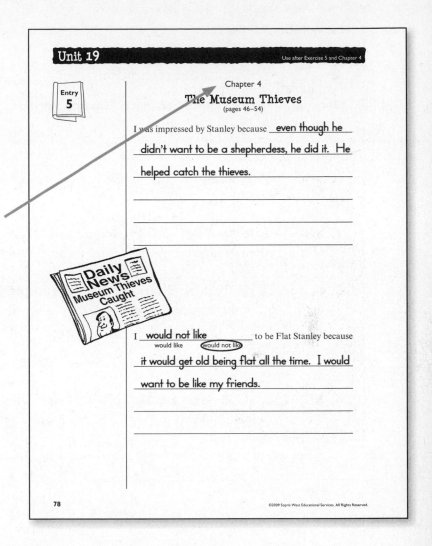

Unit 19 — Use after Exercise 5 and Chapter 4

Entry 5

Chapter 4
The Museum Thieves
(pages 46–54)

I was impressed by Stanley because ___even though he__
__didn't want to be a shepherdess, he did it. He__
__helped catch the thieves.__

I ___would not like___ to be Flat Stanley because
would like / would not like
__it would get old being flat all the time. I would__
__want to be like my friends.__

78

©2009 Sopris West Educational Services. All Rights Reserved.

PROCEDURES

For each step, demonstrate and guide practice, as needed. Then have students complete the page independently.

Personal Response: Opinion, Sentence Writing—Specific Instructions

- Have students complete the sentence starters with their own opinions. Remind them to start sentences with a capital and end with a period.
- Think aloud with students and discuss possible answers, as needed.

Self-monitoring

Have students check and correct their work.

STORY COMPREHENSION • SEQUENCE OF EVENTS

COMPREHENSION PROCESSES
Remember, Understand

WRITING TRAITS
Organization—Sequencing
Conventions—Complete Sentence, Capital, Period
Presentation

PROCEDURES
For each step, demonstrate and guide practice, as needed. Then have students complete the page independently.

1. **Selection Response—Basic Instructions** (Item 1)
   Have students read the question and fill in the bubble for the correct answer.

2. **Sequence of Events: Chart, Sentence Completion—Basic Instructions** (Item 2)
   • Have students read the directions and sentence starters, then fill in the blanks to complete the sequence of events. Remind students to put a period at the end of each sentence.
   • Think aloud with students and discuss possible answers, as needed.

3. **Sequence of Events: Paragraph Writing—Basic Instructions** (Item 3)
   Have students read the instructions and write a paragraph using the events from the graphic organizer.
   Remind students to start sentences with a capital and end with a period.

Identifying—Setting

Using Graphic Organizer
Identifying—Events

Sequencing
Explaining—Events

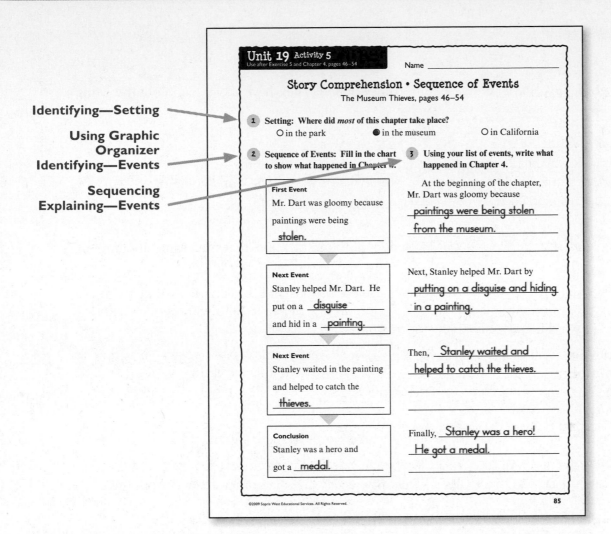

Unit 19 Activity 5
Use after Exercise 5 and Chapter 4, pages 46–54

Name _____

Story Comprehension • Sequence of Events
The Museum Thieves, pages 46–54

1 Setting: Where did *most* of this chapter take place?
- ○ in the park
- ● in the museum
- ○ in California

2 Sequence of Events: Fill in the chart to show what happened in Chapter 4.

3 Using your list of events, write what happened in Chapter 4.

First Event
Mr. Dart was gloomy because paintings were being **stolen.**

At the beginning of the chapter, Mr. Dart was gloomy because _paintings were being stolen from the museum._

Next Event
Stanley helped Mr. Dart. He put on a **disguise** and hid in a **painting.**

Next, Stanley helped Mr. Dart by _putting on a disguise and hiding in a painting._

Next Event
Stanley waited in the painting and helped to catch the **thieves.**

Then, _Stanley waited and helped to catch the thieves._

Conclusion
Stanley was a hero and got a **medal.**

Finally, _Stanley was a hero! He got a medal._

85

❶ SOUND REVIEW

❷ SHIFTY WORD BLENDING

For each word, have students say the underlined sound. Then have them sound out the word smoothly and say it. Use the words in sentences, as appropriate.

❸ ACCURACY AND FLUENCY BUILDING
- For each task, have students say any underlined part, then read the word.
- Set a pace. Then have students read the whole words in each task and column.
- Provide repeated practice, building accuracy first, then fluency.

D1. Rhyming Words
Have students read each set of rhyming words and identify what's the same about them.

E1. Tricky Words
- For each Tricky Word, have students use the sounds and word parts they know to silently sound out the word. Use the word in a sentence to help with pronunciation.
- If the word is unfamiliar, tell students the word.

terribly	He was very, very unhappy. He was . . . *terribly* . . . unhappy.
soldiers	The members of an army are called . . . *soldiers.*
course	The soldiers ran an obstacle . . . *course.*
rough	The opposite of smooth is . . . *rough.*

- Have students go back and read the whole words in the column.

E2. Rhyming Tricky Words
Have students read the words and identify what's the same about them. Use the words in sentences, as needed.

brought	She didn't rent a pool towel. She . . . *brought* . . . her own.
thought	We didn't go swimming. We . . . *thought* . . . it was too cold.
ought	He should do it. He . . . *ought* . . . to do it.

❹ MULTISYLLABIC WORDS

For each word, have students read the syllables, then the whole word. Use the word in a sentence, as appropriate.

pajama	We wore our nightclothes to the . . . *pajama* . . . party.
models	Mr. Enright's son enjoys making airplane . . . *models.*
signal	When the teacher turns the lights off, it is a . . . *signal* . . . to stop.
pleasant	If something is nice, you can say it is . . . *pleasant.*
regular	Something that is ordinary is . . . *regular.*
religion	People who believe in a god practice a . . . *religion.*

❺ MORPHOGRAPHS AND AFFIXES
- Have students read the underlined part, then the word.
- Repeat practice with whole words, mixing group and individual turns. Build accuracy, then fluency.

❻ GENERALIZATION: READING NEW WORDS IN PARAGRAPHS

Flat Stanley

Unit 19 Exercise 6
Use before Chapter 5

1. SOUND REVIEW Use selected Sound Cards from Units 1–19.

2. SHIFTY WORD BLENDING For each word, have students say the underlined part, sound out smoothly, then read the word.

| sh<u>a</u>me | sh<u>a</u>ke | sh<u>oo</u>k | sh<u>oo</u>t | sh<u>ou</u>t |

3. ACCURACY/FLUENCY BUILDING For each column, have students say any underlined part, then read each word. Next, have them read the column.

A1 Mixed Practice	**B1** Word Endings	**C1** Word Endings	**D1** Rhyming Words	**E1** Tricky Words
<u>kn</u>elt	clamp<u>ed</u>	tire	treasure	terribly
bul<u>ged</u>	rud<u>er</u>	tiring	measure	soldiers
t<u>oy</u>s	kiss<u>ed</u>		pleasure	course
burst	whoosh<u>ing</u>	notice		rough
t<u>oa</u>sts	event<u>s</u>	noticing	rummage	**E2** Rhyming Tricky Words
crept			storage	
hurts		dry	garbage	brought
str<u>o</u>de		dried		thought
<u>fu</u>rther				ought

ENTHUSIASM

Make a special effort to acknowledge what students can do.

Say things like: You can read multisyllabic words without help from adults.

You can figure out words you've never seen before.

You can read and use snazzy words like: *terribly, regular,* and *rough* . . . That is very impressive.

4. MULTISYLLABIC WORDS Have students read each word part, then read each whole word.

A	pa•ja•ma	pajama	mod•els	models
B	sig•nal	signal	pleas•ant	pleasant
C	reg•u•lar	regular	re•li•gion	religion

5. MORPHOGRAPHS AND AFFIXES Have students read the underlined part, then the word.

| occa<u>sion</u> | clever<u>ness</u> | enjoy<u>able</u> | <u>dis</u>like | <u>im</u>portant |

6. GENERALIZATION Have students read the paragraph silently, then out loud. (New words: Agnes, flung, skip)

The day of the big party had arrived, and Agnes was late. The chocolate cake she baked had taken a long time to decorate. She had to rummage around in her closet to find something to wear. She flung clothes out of her closet. She even had to toss out an old bicycle tire. She was getting discouraged and almost decided to skip the party. At last! She found the perfect dress!

60

COMPREHENSION PROCESSES
Apply

PROCEDURES
Introducing Vocabulary

★ enough is enough ★ pleasant ★ perhaps ★ rummage ★ strode ★ ought ★ occasion ★ cleverness

- For each vocabulary word, have students read the word by parts, then read the whole word.
- Read the student-friendly explanations to students as they follow with their fingers. Then have students use the vocabulary word by following the gray text.
- Review and discuss the illustrations.

  Note: Student vocabulary pages for this unit are found in the students' *Exercise Book 3*.

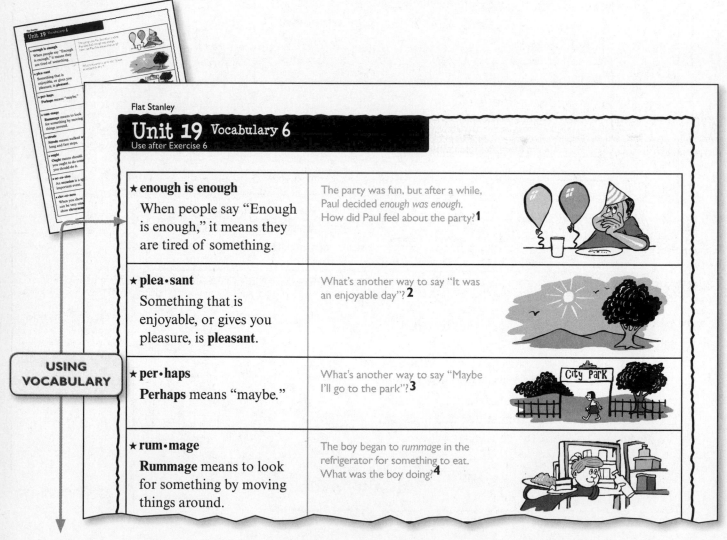

Flat Stanley

Unit 19 Vocabulary 6
Use after Exercise 6

★ **enough is enough** When people say "Enough is enough," it means they are tired of something.	The party was fun, but after a while, Paul decided *enough was enough.* How did Paul feel about the party?**1**
★ **plea•sant** Something that is enjoyable, or gives you pleasure, is **pleasant**.	What's another way to say "It was an enjoyable day"?**2**
★ **per•haps** **Perhaps** means "maybe."	What's another way to say "Maybe I'll go to the park"?**3**
★ **rum•mage** **Rummage** means to look for something by moving things around.	The boy began to *rummage* in the refrigerator for something to eat. What was the boy doing?**4**

USING VOCABULARY

❶ **Apply:** Using Idioms and Expressions—enough is enough (Paul was tired of the party.)

❷ **Apply:** Using Vocabulary—pleasant (It was a pleasant day.)

❸ **Apply:** Using Vocabulary—perhaps (Perhaps I'll go to the park.)

❹ **Apply:** Using Vocabulary—rummage (The boy was moving things around to look in the refrigerator.)

★ = New in this unit

USING VOCABULARY

★ **strode** **Strode** means walked with long and fast steps.	What's another way to say "The boy *strode* through the crowd"?**1**	
★ **ought** **Ought** means should. If you ought to do something, you should do it.	Dad decided he *ought* to get more exercise. Use the word *ought* to tell me what you should do. **2**	
★ **oc·ca·sion** An **occasion** is a special or important event.	What *occasion* do we celebrate once a year with cake and ice cream?**3**	
★ **clev·er·ness** When you show that you can be very smart, you show **cleverness**.	Through *cleverness*, Stanley solved the case. Stanley showed . . . **4**	

61

❶ **Apply:** Using Vocabulary—strode (The boy walked with long and fast steps through the crowd.)

❷ **Apply:** Using Vocabulary—ought (I ought to get up earlier in the morning.)

❸ **Apply:** Using Vocabulary—occasion (We celebrate my birthday. My birthday is a special occasion.)

❹ **Apply:** Using Vocabulary—cleverness (cleverness)

USING VOCABULARY

Be enthusiastic about learning new words. Keep a running list of words you would like to use and encourage students to use. Keep the list handy when you are teaching. Put students' names on the board to acknowledge use of a word. Say things like:
[Amy] used the word *pleasant* when she talked about the picnic we had. What a great way to use a vocabulary word!

CHAPTER 5 INSTRUCTIONS

Students read pages 55–60 with the teacher and pages 60–65 on their own.
Page 60 is split between the two reading sections.

Note: If you're working on a 9- to 12-Day Plan, you will read pages
60–65 with students.

COMPREHENSION PROCESSES

Remember, Understand, Apply, Evaluate

PROCEDURES

> **PREP NOTE**
> Students will stop and start reading in the middle of pages 39, 49, and 60. Mark those places in students' books with a sticky note.

1. **Reviewing Chapter 4, pages 49–53**

   Summarizing—Events; Inferring; Using Vocabulary—furious; Explaining—End/Conclusion

   Discuss the questions from the previous Setting a Purpose.
   Say something like:
   Yesterday, you read pages 49–53 on your own. Let's see what you found out.
   What would the thieves do to anyone who tried to capture them? (They would kill them.)
   Why did Stanley yell? What did he yell? (He was furious. His plan was to call for the police when he saw the thieves. He yelled "Police! The sneak thieves are here.")
   What happened to the thieves? (They were arrested.)
   What happened at the end of the chapter? (Stanley got a medal and his picture in the paper.)

2. **Introducing Chapter 5**

   Identifying—Title; Using Vocabulary—jealous; Inferring; Predicting

   What's the title of the chapter? (Arthur's Good Idea)
   How do you think Arthur felt when Stanley got the medal and helped catch the thieves?
   (He was probably jealous.)
   I wonder if he also felt a little proud. What do you think? (He was probably proud too.)
   Given the title of this chapter, what do you think might happen?
   (Arthur will figure out how to get Stanley back to normal.)

3. **First Reading**

   • Ask questions and discuss the story as indicated by the blue text in this guide.
   • Mix group and individual turns, independent of your voice.
     Have students work toward a group accuracy goal of 0–6 errors.
     Quietly keep track of errors made by all students in the group.
   • After reading the story, practice any difficult words.
     Repeat if students have not reached the accuracy goal.

4. **Second Reading, Timed Readings: Repeated Reading**

   • As time allows, have students do Timed Readings while others follow along.
   • Time individuals for 30 seconds and encourage each child to work for a personal best.
   • Determine words correct per minute. Record student scores.

ARTHUR'S GOOD IDEA

For a while Stanley Lambchop was a famous name. Everywhere that Stanley went, people stared and pointed at him. He could hear them whisper, "Over there, Agnes, over there! That must be Stanley Lambchop, the one who caught the sneak thieves . . ." and things like that.

But after a few weeks the whispering and

55

After Reading Page 55

❶ **Apply:** Inferring, Explaining
Why did people point at Stanley and stare at him?
(He had caught the thieves. He was famous.)

❷ **Evaluate:** Responding; **Apply:** Explaining
Do you think being famous was fun? Why or why not?
(Yes, it was fun. Getting attention is always fun. No, I wouldn't like having people point and stare at me . . .)

the staring stopped. People had other things to think about. Stanley did not mind. Being famous had been fun, but enough was enough.

And then came a further change, and it was not a pleasant one. People began to laugh and make fun of him as he passed by. "Hello, Super-Skinny!" they would shout, and even ruder things, about the way he looked.

Stanley told his parents how he felt. "It's the other kids I mostly mind," he said. "They don't like me anymore because I'm different. Flat."

"Shame on them," Mrs. Lambchop said. "It is wrong to dislike people for their shapes. Or their religion, for that matter, or the color of their skin."

56

"I know," Stanley said. "Only maybe it's impossible for everybody to like *everybody*."

"Perhaps," said Mrs. Lambchop. "But they can try."

Later that night Arthur Lambchop was woken by the sound of crying. In the darkness he crept across the room and knelt by Stanley's bed.

"Are you okay?" he said.

"Go away," Stanley said.

"Don't be mad at me," Arthur said. "You're still mad because I let you get tangled the day you were my kite, I guess."

"Skip it, will you?" Stanley said. "I'm not mad. Go away."

"Please let's be friends. . . ." Arthur couldn't help crying a little, too. "Oh, Stanley," he

57

After Reading Page 57

❶ **Apply:** Defining and Using Idioms and Expressions—enough was enough
The book says, "Being famous was fun, but enough was enough." What does that mean?
(Stanley was tired of all the attention. He had had enough attention.)

❷ **Understand:** Explaining
Why did the kids tease Stanley?
(He was flat. He was different. They were mean.)

said. "Please tell me what's wrong."

Stanley waited for a long time before he spoke. "The thing is," he said, "I'm just not happy anymore. I'm tired of being flat. I want to be a regular shape again, like other people. But I'll have to go on being flat forever. It makes me sick."

"Oh, Stanley," Arthur said. He dried his tears on a corner of Stanley's sheet and could think of nothing more to say.

"Don't talk about what I just said," Stanley told him. "I don't want the folks to worry. That would only make it worse."

"You're brave," Arthur said. "You really are."

He took hold of Stanley's hand. The two brothers sat together in the darkness, being

58

After Reading Page 58

❶ **Understand:** Explaining
Why was Stanley upset?
(He was tired of being flat. He wanted to be normal.)

❷ **Apply:** Inferring, Explaining
Why did Stanley say, "Don't talk about what I just said"?
(He didn't want to worry his parents.)

friends. They were both still sad, but each one felt a *little* better than he had before.

And then, suddenly, though he was not even trying to think, Arthur had an idea. He jumped up and turned on the light and ran to the big storage box where toys and things were kept. He began to rummage in the box.

Stop Reading Here

Stanley sat up in bed to watch.

Arthur flung aside a football and some lead soldiers and airplane models and lots of wooden blocks, and then he said, "Aha!" He had found what he wanted—an old bicycle pump. He held it up, and Stanley and he looked at each other.

"Okay," Stanley said at last. "But take it easy." He put the end of the long pump hose in his mouth and clamped his lips tightly

60

After Reading Page 60 (top half)

❶ **Remember:** Identifying—What
What is Arthur doing?
(He is rummaging through a box of toys and things.)

❷ **Create:** Generating ideas
Arthur wants to help Stanley be a regular shape again. What do you think his idea is?
(He's going to find something to help flat Stanley not be flat. He's going to find something to blow him up . . . maybe a bicycle pump or something.)

CHAPTER 5 INSTRUCTIONS

Students read pages 60–65 without the teacher, independently or with partners. Page 60 is split between reading sections.

Note: If you're working on a 9- to 12-day plan, you will read pages 60–65 with students.

COMPREHENSION PROCESSES

Remember, Understand

PROCEDURES

1. Getting Ready

Have students turn to page 60.

2. Setting a Purpose

Identifying—Problem, Solution, What; Explaining; Using Vocabulary—absurd

Before beginning, say something like:

As you read the rest of the chapter, try to answer the following questions:

- What was Stanley's problem?
- What was Arthur's idea?
- What was absurd in the chapter?
- Why did the Lambchops celebrate at the end of the book?

> **PREP NOTE**
>
> **Setting a Purpose**
> Write questions on a chalkboard, white board, or large piece of paper before working with your small group.

3. Reading on Your Own: Partner or Whisper Reading

- Have students take turns reading every other page with a partner or have students whisper read pages 60–65 on their own.
  Say something like:
  Everyone, put your finger on the third paragraph on page 60. It starts, "Arthur flung aside . . . "
  This is where you're going to start reading on your own—without me.
  Now turn to page 65. This is the end and where you will stop reading.

- Continue having students track each word with their fingers.

4. Comprehension and Skill Work

For students on a 7-Day Plan, tell them that they will work on their Book Journal and do Comprehension and Skill Activity 6 after they read on their own. Guide practice, as needed. For teacher directions, see pages 101 and 102. (For 9- to 12-Day Plans, see the Lesson Planner, page 9.)

5. Homework 6: New Passage

Start Reading Here

friends. They were both still sad, but each one felt a *little* better than he had before.

And then, suddenly, though he was not even trying to think, Arthur had an idea. He jumped up and turned on the light and ran to the big storage box where toys and things were kept. He began to rummage in the box.

Stanley sat up in bed to watch.

Arthur flung aside a football and some lead soldiers and airplane models and lots of wooden blocks, and then he said, "Aha!" He had found what he wanted—an old bicycle pump. He held it up, and Stanley and he looked at each other.

"Okay," Stanley said at last. "But take it easy." He put the end of the long pump hose in his mouth and clamped his lips tightly

60

about it so that no air could escape.

"I'll go slowly," Arthur said. "If it hurts or anything, wiggle your hand at me."

He began to pump. At first nothing happened except that Stanley's cheeks bulged a bit. Arthur watched his hand, but there was no wiggle signal, so he pumped on. Then, suddenly, Stanley's top half began to swell.

"It's working! It's working!" shouted Arthur, pumping away.

Stanley spread his arms so that the air could get around inside him more easily. He got bigger and bigger. The buttons of his pajama top burst off—*Pop! Pop! Pop!* A moment more and he was all rounded out; head and body, arms and legs. But not his right foot. That foot stayed flat.

61

Arthur stopped pumping. "It's like trying to do the very last bit of those long balloons," he said. "Maybe a shake would help."

Stanley shook his right foot twice, and with a little *whooshing* sound it swelled out to match the left one. There stood Stanley Lambchop as he used to be, as if he had never been flat at all.

"Thank you, Arthur," Stanley said. "Thank you very much."

The brothers were shaking hands when Mr. Lambchop strode into the room with Mrs. Lambchop right behind him. "We heard you!" said Mr. Lambchop. "Up and talking when you ought to be asleep, eh? Shame on—"

"GEORGE!" said Mrs. Lambchop.

63

"Stanley's *round* again!"

"You're right!" said Mr. Lambchop, noticing. "Good for you, Stanley!"

"I'm the one who did it," Arthur said. "I blew him up."

Everyone was terribly excited and happy, of course. Mrs. Lambchop made hot chocolate to celebrate the occasion, and several toasts were drunk to Arthur for his cleverness.

When the little party was over, Mr. and Mrs. Lambchop tucked the boys back into their beds and kissed them, and then they turned out the light. "Good night," they said.

"Good night," said Stanley and Arthur.

It had been a long and tiring day. Very soon all the Lambchops were asleep.

65

ENTRY 6

COMPREHENSION PROCESSES
Understand, Create, Evaluate

WRITING TRAITS
Ideas and Content
Word Choice
Conventions—Complete Sentence, Capital, Period
Presentation

Responding; Generating Ideas
Sentence Completion
Using Vocabulary—adventure

Responding, Generating Ideas
Asking Questions

Unit 19   Use after Exercise 6 and Chapter 5

Entry 6

Chapter 5
Arthur's Good Idea

Stanley had many adventures. The one I like best was
when Stanley caught the thieves

because he had to dress up like a girl, and I
thought that was funny.

Would you recommend this book to other kids your age? (yes)   no

What would you tell a friend about this book? It is a great book. You will
enjoy reading about Stanley.

Would you like to read more books about Flat Stanley? (yes)   no

What question would you like to ask the author, Jeff Brown?
How did you come up with the idea of making Flat Stanley flat?

©2009 Sopris West Educational Services. All Rights Reserved.   79

PROCEDURES
For each step, demonstrate and guide practice, as needed. Then have students complete the page independently.

1. **Personal Response: Opinion—Specific Instructions**
   • Have students complete the sentence starter with their own opinions. Remind them to start sentences with a capital and end with a period.
   • Think aloud with students and discuss possible answers, as needed.

2. **Personal Response: Yes/No—Basic Instructions**
   Have students evaluate the story and respond "yes" or "no" to the first and third questions.

3. **Personal Response: Sentence Writing—Specific Instructions**
   Have students write a complete sentence response to the second question.

4. **Personal Response: Asking Questions—Specific Instructions**
   Have students generate and write a question they would like to ask the author. Remind them to use a question mark at the end of the question.

Self-monitoring
Have students check and correct their work.

Note: The last page of My Book Journal is a list of other books by Jeff Brown that the children might enjoy reading.

CROSSWORD PUZZLE

COMPREHENSION PROCESSES

Remember, Understand

PROCEDURES

For each step, demonstrate and guide practice, as needed. Then have students complete the page independently.

Vocabulary: Sentence Completion—Specific Instructions

- Tell students that they will complete a crossword puzzle. Say something like:
Today, you get to do a crossword puzzle. A crossword puzzle has blanks for words that go down the page and across the page.

- Have students read the words in the word bank. Then have students read the sentences and fill in the blanks with words from the bank. Say something like:
Put your finger on the box that says "Word Bank." Read the words.
(disguise, sensational, alter, absurd, recently, unique)
Now, let's complete each of the sentences with the correct word from the word bank.
Read sentence one. (We *blank* read a book about Flat Stanley.)
Look at the word bank. When did we read *Flat Stanley*? (recently)
Read the sentence with the word *recently* to see if it makes sense.
(We *recently* read a book about Flat Stanley.)
Does that make sense? (yes) *Recently* will be number one in the word puzzle.
Look at the label above the sentence. Now look at the puzzle.
Will the word go down or across? (down)
Find it on the puzzle and cross out the word *recently* in the word bank.

Read Item 2. (He was *blank* because he was as flat as a pancake.)
Look at the word bank. What word belongs in the blank? (unique)
Let's read the sentence with that word to see if it makes sense.
(He was *unique* because he was as flat as a pancake.) Does that make sense? (yes)
So what will you do next? (Write the word in the puzzle.)
Then cross the word out in the . . . word bank.
Will the word *unique* be written down or across? (down)

- Repeat for items 3–6, as needed.
- Have students write the correct words in the crossword puzzle.

Identifying—What
Using Vocabulary—
disguise, sensational,
alter, absurd,
recently, unique

Unit 19 Activity 6
Use after Exercise 6 and Chapter 5

Name _____

Crossword Puzzle

Flat Stanley

Fill in the blanks using words from the word bank. Use the words from the word bank to complete the crossword puzzle.

Down

1. We __recently__ read a book about Flat Stanley.

2. He was __unique__ because he was flat as a pancake.

3. *Flat Stanley* has many unbelievable or __absurd__ events.

Across

4. Stanley became famous when he helped catch the museum thieves.

   The story was __sensational__.

5. Stanley wore a __disguise__ and dressed like a shepherdess.

6. Stanley had to __alter__ his looks so the thieves wouldn't see him.

Word Bank
disguise
sensational
alter
absurd
recently
unique

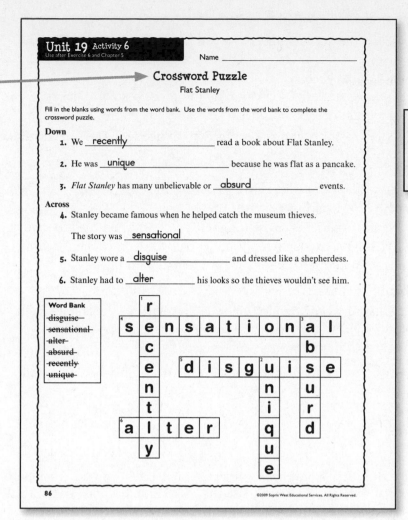

86   ©2009 Sopris West Educational Services. All Rights Reserved.

❶ SOUND REVIEW

Have students read the sounds and key word phrases. Work for accuracy, then fluency.

❷ SOUND PRACTICE

- For each task, have students spell and say the focus sound in the gray bar.
- Next, have students read each underlined sound, the word, then the whole column.
- Repeat with each column, building accuracy first, then fluency.

❸ SHIFTY WORD BLENDING

❹ ACCURACY AND FLUENCY BUILDING

- For each task, have students say any underlined part, then read the word.
- Set a pace. Then have students read the whole words in each task and column.
- Provide repeated practice, building accuracy first, then fluency.

C1. Multisyllabic Words

- For the list of words divided by syllables, have students read each syllable, then the whole word. Use the word in a sentence, as appropriate.
- For the list of whole words, build accuracy and then fluency.

Penelope	The main character in today's story is a girl named . . . *Penelope.*
tingle	When I get scared, my toes . . . *tingle.*
pizzazz	Someone who is exciting has . . . *pizzazz.*
pufferfish	One kind of fish on the Great Barrier Reef is the . . . *pufferfish.*

D1. Tricky Words

- For each Tricky Word, have students use the sounds and word parts they know to silently sound out the word. Use the word in a sentence to help with pronunciation.

mirror
Look at the first word. Silently sound out the word, then thumbs up. Use my sentence to help you. You can see your own reflection in a . . . *mirror.*
Read the word three times. (mirror, mirror, mirror)

trouble	Follow the rules and you won't get into . . . *trouble.*
sorry	When I accidentally bumped Andrew, I said, "I'm . . . *sorry.*"
early	Megan gets up at 4 a.m. That is very . . . *early.*

- Have students go back and read the whole words in the column.

❺ WORD ENDINGS

Have students read any underlined word, then the word with an ending.
Note: Tell students to note the spelling changes when endings are added to the words in Row B.

❻ MORPHOGRAPHS AND AFFIXES

- Have students read the underlined part, then the word.
- Repeat practice with whole words, mixing group and individual turns.
  Build accuracy, then fluency.

Flat Stanley

Unit 19 Exercise 7
Use before Fluency

1. SOUND REVIEW Have students review sounds for accuracy, then for fluency.

A	ph as in phone	OW as in snow	aw as in paw	ea as in bread	gi as in giraffe
B	ue	oy	ge	kn	oi

2. SOUND PRACTICE In each column, have students spell and say the sound, next say any underlined sound and the word, then read the column.

au	-dge	oa	u
h<u>au</u>l	tru<u>dge</u>	t<u>oa</u>sts	g<u>u</u>lp
<u>Au</u>gust	bu<u>dge</u>	m<u>oa</u>ned	sp<u>u</u>nk
s<u>au</u>cers	we<u>dge</u>	<u>oa</u>tmeal	b<u>u</u>lged

3. SHIFTY WORD BLENDING For each word, have students say the underlined part, sound out smoothly, then read the word.

st<u>uff</u>	p<u>uff</u>	p<u>oo</u>f	g<u>oo</u>f	g<u>oo</u>p

4. ACCURACY/FLUENCY BUILDING For each column, have students say any underlined part, then read each word. Next, have them read the column.

A1 Mixed Practice	B1 Mixed Review	C1 Multisyllabic Words		D1 Tricky Words
fl<u>a</u>kes	stairs	Pe·nel·o·pe	Penelope	mirror
p<u>o</u>ke	board	tin·gle	tingle	trouble
b<u>ow</u>l	nurse	piz·zazz	pizzazz	sorry
silv<u>er</u>	silly	puf·fer·fish	pufferfish	early

5. WORD ENDINGS Have students read any underlined word, then the word with an ending.

A	<u>grumbl</u>ed	<u>flash</u>y	<u>wok</u>en

B	prickle	prickly	spike	spiky	bore	boring

6. MORPHOGRAPHS AND AFFIXES Have students read each underlined word part, then the word.

norma<u>l</u>	cheerful<u>ly</u>	speech<u>less</u>	absolute<u>ly</u>

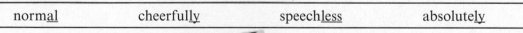

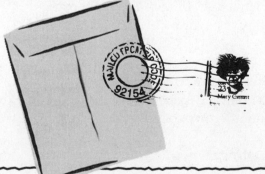

> **GRADUALLY INCREASE STUDENT RESPONSE RATE (Reminder)**
>
> After students are accurate, gradually increase the rate of response. Demonstrate and guide a pace slightly faster than the students' rate.

FLUENCY PASSAGE INSTRUCTIONS

This Story Reading targets fluency as the primary goal of instruction and practice. Students do repeated readings of this poem to improve accuracy, expression, and rate.

Note: The fluency passage is found in *Exercise Book 3*, Unit 19, Fluency, on pages 63 and 64.

PROCEDURES

1. **Warm-Up: Partner Reading or Whisper Reading**

   Before beginning group Story Reading, have students finger track and partner or whisper read the selection.

2. **First Reading**
   - Mix group and individual turns, independent of your voice.
     Have students work toward a group accuracy goal of 0–5 errors.
     Quietly keep track of errors made by all students in the group.
   - After reading the story, practice any difficult words.
     Reread the story if students have not reached the accuracy goal.

3. **Second Reading, Short Passage Practice: Developing Prosody**
   - Demonstrate reading the first stanza with expression and fluency.
     Have students finger track as you read.
   - Have students choral read the first stanza. Encourage reading with expression and fluency.
   - Repeat with the second stanza.

4. **Third Reading, Group Timed Readings: Repeated Reading**

   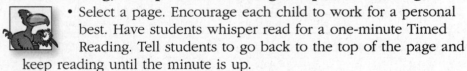
   - Select a page. Encourage each child to work for a personal best. Have students whisper read for a one-minute Timed Reading. Tell students to go back to the top of the page and keep reading until the minute is up.
   - Have students put their finger on the last word they read and count the number of words read correctly in one minute.
   - Have students do a second Timed Reading of the same page.
   - Have students try to beat their last score.
   - Celebrate improvements.

5. **Written Assessment (Comprehension and Skill)**

   Tell students they will do a Written Assessment after they read "Prickly Penelope." (For teacher directions, see pages 109–111.)

6. **Homework 7: Repeated Reading**

Flat Stanley

Unit 19 Fluency (1 of 2)
Use after Exercise 7

Prickly Penelope
by Ann Watanabe
illustrated by Eldon Doty

Be Careful What You Wish For

"Wake up, Penelope," called Mom. "It's time for school." 9

"Not yet," moaned Penelope. Penelope absolutely did not like 18
getting up early. She slowly rolled out of bed, changed into her school 31
clothes, and looked in the mirror. 37

Penelope grumbled, "I don't like my flat hair. I wish it were spiky. 50
I don't like these boring clothes. I wish they were flashy!" 61

Penelope grabbed her backpack and trudged down the stairs. She 71
sat down at the table and stared at her breakfast. "That oatmeal is 84
boring," she said. "It is a bowl of goop. I want oatmeal with spunk. I 99
want a bowl of spiky flakes that hop 107
and pop. I want a meal with 114
pizzazz." 115

Penelope's older brother 118
bounded into the room. "Good 123
morning," he said cheerfully. 127

"What are you so happy about?" 133
snapped Penelope. 135

Mom said, "Penelope, you need 140
to stop being so grumpy. You are 147
almost prickly." 149

63

Flat Stanley

Unit 19 Fluency (2 of 2)

"Ha! She is prickly—Prickly Penelope," said her brother. Then he laughed. | 11
| 12

"Prickly!" said Penelope. "I like being prickly. If I could, I would be prickly like a pufferfish! I could blow up and prickle you." | 24
| 36

All of a sudden, the oatmeal started hopping and popping in the bowl. Penelope's body started to tingle. Her flat hair turned spiky. Her boring clothes turned flashy. Penelope's eyes bulged and her mouth opened wide. She took a huge gulp of air. Poof! She puffed up like a pufferfish. Sharp silver spikes poked through her clothes. | 48
| 59
| 69
| 83
| 93

"Prickly Penelope is a pufferfish!" yelled her brother. | 101

He was right. Penelope's body had puffed into a huge ball. Spines stuck out through her clothes. Penelope couldn't believe what was happening. Her eyes were as big as saucers. For a moment, she was speechless! | 113
| 123
| 136
| 137

"Oh my," said Mom. "You are a prickly pufferfish. You got what you wished for!" | 149
| 152

Penelope said, "I am sorry for being so prickly. I will never be grumpy again. I love my hair. I love my clothes. I love my brother. I love being me." | 158
| 165
| 172
| 179
| 183

Poof! Penelope was back to her normal self. And from that day on, she was never prickly again. | 189
| 196
| 201

What lesson did Penelope learn?

WRITTEN ASSESSMENT (1 of 3)

COMPREHENSION PROCESSES

Remember, Understand, Apply

WRITING TRAITS

Conventions—Complete Sentence, Capital, Period
Presentation

Test Taking

Unit 19 Written Assessment
Use after Exercise 7 and Prickly Penelope

WARM-UP

Antone	antennas	bacon	spotless

Antone's Absurd Adventure

Antone didn't like chores. Today he had to clean out the hot, dusty shed. Instead of sweeping, he took a break behind the shed where his mother couldn't see him. He noticed a trail of ants and lay down to watch.

Antone marveled at how hard the little ants worked. Just watching them made him tired.

Suddenly, Antone got smaller, and antennas sprouted from his head. Before he could panic, he was jostled by one of the ants. "No time to dawdle," said the ant.

"But I'm not an ant," Antone said in his most polite voice. "Ordinarily, I'm a boy."

"Perhaps you were a boy," the ant replied, "but now you're an ant. Back to work!"

Antone led the ants to the garbage can where he knew they would find leftovers from breakfast. As he lifted a big chunk of bacon, he was jostled again. "Back to work!" He recognized the voice. "Wake up," said his mother.

Antone sat up and counted his arms and legs—only two of each! He marched back into the shed and worked like an ant until it was spotless. Antone had learned a good lesson from his adventure as an ant.

continued →

WRITTEN ASSESSMENT (2 of 3)

Using Graphic Organizer (Chart)
Sequencing; Identifying—Events

Summarizing; Sequencing—Events
Sentence Writing; Paragraph Writing

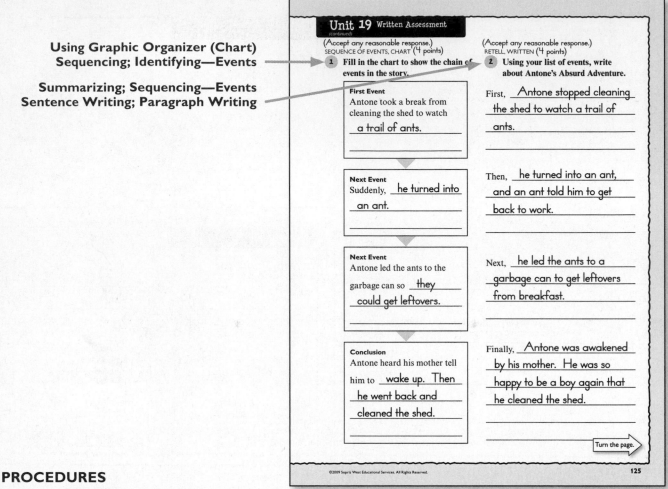

Unit 19 Written Assessment
(continued)

(Accept any reasonable response.)
SEQUENCE OF EVENTS, CHART (4 points)

1 Fill in the chart to show the chain of events in the story.

First Event
Antone took a break from cleaning the shed to watch _a trail of ants._

Next Event
Suddenly, _he turned into an ant._

Next Event
Antone led the ants to the garbage can so _they could get leftovers._

Conclusion
Antone heard his mother tell him to _wake up. Then he went back and cleaned the shed._

(Accept any reasonable response.)
RETELL, WRITTEN (4 points)

2 Using your list of events, write about Antone's Absurd Adventure.

First, _Antone stopped cleaning the shed to watch a trail of ants._

Then, _he turned into an ant, and an ant told him to get back to work._

Next, _he led the ants to a garbage can to get leftovers from breakfast._

Finally, _Antone was awakened by his mother. He was so happy to be a boy again that he cleaned the shed._

Turn the page.

125

PROCEDURES

Do not demonstrate or guide practice.

Written Assessment—Basic Instructions

1. Introduce the Written Assessment.
   - Tell students that their work today is an opportunity for them to show what they can do independently. Say something like:
     You should be very proud of your accomplishments. Remember, on a Written Assessment, you get to show me what you can do all by yourself.

   - Tell students they will whisper read the passage and then answer the questions without help.

2. Check for student understanding. Say something like:
   Look at your assessment. What are you going to do first? (write my name)
   What are you going to do next? (whisper read the passage)
   What will you do after you read the passage? (answer the questions)
   That's great. Now what will you do if you get to a hard question?
   (reread the question sind try again)
   That's right. What should you do if it's still hard? (reread the passage and try again)
   Very good. And if you still aren't sure, what will you do? (do my best and keep going)

WRITTEN ASSESSMENT (3 of 3)

Inferring; Using Vocabulary—absurd

Inferring—Lesson

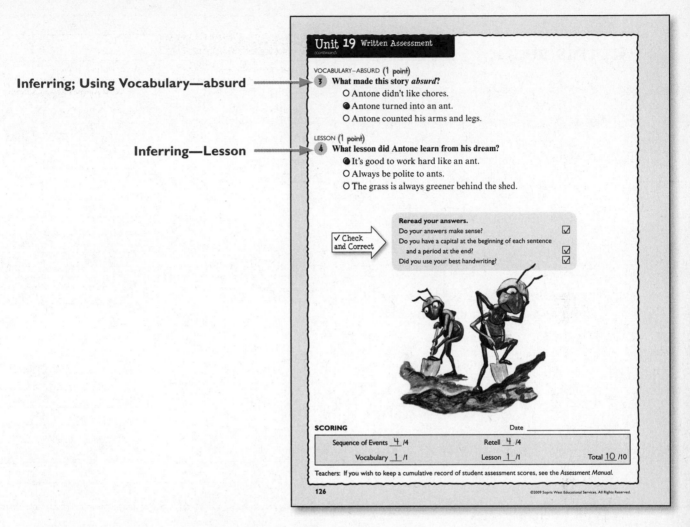

Unit 19 Written Assessment
(continued)

VOCABULARY—ABSURD (1 point)
3 **What made this story *absurd*?**
 O Antone didn't like chores.
 ● Antone turned into an ant.
 O Antone counted his arms and legs.

LESSON (1 point)
4 **What lesson did Antone learn from his dream?**
 ● It's good to work hard like an ant.
 O Always be polite to ants.
 O The grass is always greener behind the shed.

✓ Check and Correct

Reread your answers.
Do your answers make sense? ☑
Do you have a capital at the beginning of each sentence
 and a period at the end? ☑
Did you use your best handwriting? ☑

SCORING Date _____

Sequence of Events 4 /4	Retell 4 /4
Vocabulary 1 /1	Lesson 1 /1 Total 10 /10

Teachers: If you wish to keep a cumulative record of student assessment scores, see the *Assessment Manual.*

126 ©2009 Sopris West Educational Services. All Rights Reserved.

3. Remind students to check and correct.
 When you finish your assessment, what should you do? (check and correct)
 That's right. Go to the top of the page. Reread the questions and make sure your answers make
 sense. Fix anything that doesn't sound right. Make sure you have an answer for every question.

4. Remind students what to do when they finish their work.

End of the Unit

In this section, you will find:

Making Decisions

As you near the end of the unit, plan to give the Written Assessment and the Oral Reading Fluency Assessment to each child in your group. Use this section as a general guide for making instructional decisions and doing diagnostic planning.

Written Assessment

The Unit 19 Written Assessment is located on page 123 of *Activity Book 3* and on the CD.

Oral Reading Fluency Assessment

The Unit 19 Oral Reading Fluency Assessment is located on page 116 of this teacher's guide and in the *Assessment Manual*.

Certificate of Achievement

Celebrate your children's accomplishments. When your students master the unit skills, send home the Certificate of Achievement.

Extra Practice Lessons

Use the Extra Practice lessons for students who need additional decoding and fluency work. Student materials can be copied from the Extra Practice blackline masters.

Making Decisions

GENERAL ASSESSMENT GUIDELINES

1. After students read Story Reading 7, "Prickly Penelope," give the group the Unit 19 Written Assessment in place of Comprehension and Skill Work. Follow the instructions on pages 109–111 of this guide.

2. While the group is completing the Written Assessment or any time during the day, administer the Oral Reading Fluency Assessment. Assess each student individually.

   Optional: Graph the results of the assessment. (See Unit 7 Teacher's Guide, pages 92 and 95.)
   • If the student's words correct per minute go up, congratulate the student.
   • If the student's words correct per minute go down, discuss the student's overall improvement and help him or her identify ways to improve for the next assessment.

3. Score oral fluency responses on the Student Assessment Record. Adhere to the scoring criteria in the *Assessment Manual*. Use a stopwatch to time how long it takes each student to read the Oral Reading Fluency Passage, and record errors.

USING WRITTEN ASSESSMENT RESULTS

Results of the Written Assessment *should not* be used to determine whether a student or group of students continues forward in the program. As long as students pass the Oral Reading Fluency Assessment, they should continue forward with the next unit.

The Written Assessment should be used to informally monitor how well students read independently and answer questions in writing. If any student has difficulty with the Written Assessment, re-administer the assessment orally.

If the student has difficulty answering the questions orally:
• Record the types of errors (e.g., main idea, sequencing, open-ended response).
• Provide explicit instruction for these types of questions during reading group, before independent work, and in tutorials, as needed.

   1) Demonstrate (or model) appropriate responses, guide practice, and provide opportunities for independent practice.

   2) For inferential questions, think aloud with students—explain how you arrive at an answer.

   3) For literal questions, teach students to reread a passage, locate information, reread the question, and respond.

USING THE ORAL READING FLUENCY RESULTS

At the end of each unit, you will need to make decisions regarding student progress. Should students go forward in the program? Does the group need Extra Practice before proceeding? Do individuals require more assistance and practice to continue working in their group? These decisions all require use of the oral reading fluency data and professional judgment. As you analyze assessment results, watch for trends and anomalies.

See the *Assessment Manual* for detailed information and instructional recommendations. General guidelines and recommendations follow:

Strong Pass ≥ 122 WCPM 0–2 errors	• Continue with the current pace of instruction. • Have students set goals. (Until students are reading approximately 180 words correct per minute, oral reading fluency continues to be an instructional goal.)
Pass 101–121 WCPM 0–2 errors	• Continue with the current pace of instruction. Consider increasing fluency practice.
No Pass ≤ 100 WCPM	• If a child scores a No Pass but has previously passed all assessments, you may wish to advance the student to the next unit, then carefully monitor the student. • If a child scores a No Pass but has previously passed all assessments, you may wish to advance the student to the next unit and also provide additional practice opportunities. (See below.) • If a child scores two consecutive No Passes or periodic No Passes, additional practice must be provided. (See below.) • If a child scores three consecutive No Passes, the student should be placed in a lower-performing group.

RED FLAG
A No Pass is a red flag. A mild early intervention can prevent an intense and time-consuming intervention in the future.

Added Practice Options for Groups
Warm-Ups:
• Begin each lesson with Partner Reading of the previous day's homework.
• Begin each day with Partner Reading of a Word Fluency from Extra Practice.
• Begin each lesson with a five-minute Fluency Booster. Place copies of the Unit 13–18 *Read Well* Homework in three-ring notebooks. Each day, have students begin Finger Tracking and Whisper Reading at Unit 13, Homework 1. At the end of five minutes, have students mark where they are in their notebooks. The next day, the goal is to read farther.
• Begin each Story Reading with a review of the previous day's story.
• After reading the story, include Short Passage Practice on a daily basis.

Extended Units: If several children begin to score No Passes or barely pass, extend the unit by adding Extra Practices 1, 2, and/or 3. Extra Practice lessons include Decoding Practice, Fluency Passage, Word Fluency, and a Comprehension and Skill Activity. (See pages 118–129 in this guide.)

Jell-Well Reviews: A Jell-Well Review is the *Read Well* term for a review of earlier units. A Jell-Well Review is a period of time taken to celebrate what children have learned and an opportunity to firm up their foundation of learning. To complete a Jell-Well Review, take the group back to the last unit for which all students scored Strong Passes. Then quickly cycle back up. See the *Assessment Manual* for how to build a Jell-Well Review.

Added Practice Options for Individual Students

Tutorials: Set up five-minute tutorials on a daily basis with an assistant, trained volunteer, or cross-age tutor. Have the tutor provide Short Passage Practice and Timed Readings or Extra Practice lessons.

Double Dose: Find ways to provide a double dose of *Read Well* instruction.
- Have the student work in his or her group *and* a lower-performing group.
- Have an instructional assistant, older student, or parent volunteer preview or review lessons.
- Have an instructional assistant provide instruction with Extra Practice lessons.
- Preview new lessons or review previous lessons.

END-OF-THE-UNIT CELEBRATION

When students pass the Oral Reading Fluency Assessment, celebrate with the Certificate of Achievement on page 117.

Note: Using the Flesch-Kincaid Grade Level readability formula, the Unit 19 Assessment has a 3.0 readability level. Readabilities are based on number of words per sentence and number of syllables per word. Adding one or two multisyllabic words can increase readability by a month or two. Though we are attending to readability for the assessments, the overriding factor is decodability.

TRICKY WORD and FOCUS SKILL WARM-UP

vacation	bulletin	seashore	clothes	polite	cheerfully

ORAL READING FLUENCY PASSAGE

The Yard Sale

★Brandon and Robert decided to have a yard sale. They   10
wanted to earn some money for a trip to the seashore.   21

Mrs. Wilson thought the sale was a great idea. She gave   32
the boys a couch, a bulletin board, and some picture frames.   43
Brandon found some old clothes in his room that were too small   55
for him.   57

The boys made a sign that said "yard sale" in big letters.   69
They cut the grass and cleaned up the yard. They set up some   82
tables. Then they put out all the things they wanted to sell.   94

The brothers were very polite to the people who came to   105
their sale. "Two dollars, please" and "thank you very much!"   115
they said cheerfully. Soon everything was gone, except for the   125
bulletin board. It was so big and heavy that no one wanted it.   138
Robert thought he would hang it on the wall above his bed.   150

ORAL READING FLUENCY	Start timing at the ★. Mark errors. Make a single slash in the text (/) at 60 seconds. If the student completes the passage in less than 60 seconds, have the student go back to the ★ and continue reading. Make a double slash (//) in the text at 60 seconds.
WCPM	Determine words correct per minute by subtracting errors from words read in 60 seconds.
STRONG PASS	The student scores no more than 2 errors on the first pass through the passage and reads 122 or more words correct per minute. Proceed to Unit 20.
PASS	The student scores no more than 2 errors on the first pass through the passage and reads 101 to 121 words correct per minute. Proceed to Unit 20.
NO PASS	The student scores 3 or more errors on the first pass through the passage and/or reads 100 or fewer words correct per minute. Provide added fluency practice with *RW2* Unit 19 Extra Practice. (Lessons follow the certificate at the end of the teacher's guide.) After the student completes the Extra Practice, retest the student.

Sensational Work!

_____

has successfully completed

Read Well 2 Unit 19 • *Flat Stanley*

with _____ words correct per minute.

Teacher Signature _____

Date _____

Sensational Work!

_____

has successfully completed

Read Well 2 Unit 19 • *Flat Stanley*

with _____ words correct per minute.

Teacher Signature _____

Date _____

PROCEDURES

1. Sound Review

Use selected Sound Cards from Units 1–19.

2. Sounding Out Smoothly

- For each word, have students say the underlined part, sound out the word smoothly, then read the whole word. Use the words in sentences, as needed.
- Have students read all the words in the row, building accuracy first, then fluency.
- Repeat practice. Mix group and individual turns, independent of your voice.

3. Accuracy and Fluency Building

- For each task, have students say any underlined part, then read each word.
- Set a pace. Then have students read the whole words in each task and column.
- Provide repeated practice, building accuracy first, then fluency.

4. Tricky Words

Have students read each row for accuracy, then fluency.

5. Multisyllabic Words

For each word, have students read each syllable out loud, then tell how many syllables are in the word. If needed, use the word in a sentence. Have students read the whole word.

6. Dictation

kite, like, line, sale, tale, whale

- Say "kite." Have students say the word. Guide students as they finger count and say the sounds. Have students touch or write the sounds, then read the word. Say something like:

The first word is **kite.** Say the word. (kite)

What's the first sound? (/k/) Touch under /k/.
What's the next sound? (/īīī/) Write /īīī/.
What's the last sound? (/t/) Touch under /t/.
Yes, the Bossy <u>E</u> at the end makes letter <u>i</u> say its name.
Read the word. (kite)

- Repeat with "like" and "line."
- Continue with the rhyming words: sale, tale, whale.

CAUTION

Your children may not need Extra Practice. Use assessment results to determine if Extra Practice is needed.

Unit 19 Decoding Practice

Name _____

1. SOUND REVIEW Use selected Sound Cards from Units 1–19.

2. SOUNDING OUT SMOOTHLY Have students say the underlined part, sound out and read each word, then read the row.

| t<u>ai</u>ls | <u>yar</u>d | <u>lea</u>ves | <u>mor</u>e |

3. ACCURACY/FLUENCY BUILDING Have students say any underlined part, then read each word. Next, have students read the column.

A1 Sound Practice	**B1** Mixed Practice	**C1** Bossy E	**D1** Buildups
<u>a</u>go	enj<u>oy</u>	lat<u>e</u>r	ch<u>ee</u>r
<u>a</u>round	<u>ex</u>tra	shap<u>e</u>s	<u>cheer</u>ful
<u>a</u>ttached	<u>exc</u>ept	pol<u>i</u>te	<u>cheerful</u>ly
A2 Compound Words	bamb<u>oo</u>	dec<u>i</u>ded	**D2** Names and Places
fisherman	<u>ch</u>ildren	infl<u>a</u>te	Benjamin
spiderweb	li<u>gh</u>tning	infl<u>a</u>table	Franklin
backflips	dr<u>a</u>gons		Japanese
seashore	m<u>e</u>tal	<u>u</u>se	Pacific
	luck<u>y</u>	<u>u</u>sed	China
		<u>u</u>seful	

4. TRICKY WORDS Have students read each row for accuracy, then fluency.

| A | been | Islands | wasn't | two | earn | 5 |
| B | early | earliest | idea | sign | dollars | 10 |

5. MULTISYLLABIC WORDS Have students read the word by parts, tell how many syllables are in the word, then read the whole word.

A	fa•mous	famous	fan•tas•tic	fantastic
B	sci•en•tist	scientist	rec•tan•gles	rectangles
C	prob•ab•ly	probably	ex•per•i•ment	experiment

6. DICTATION Say the word. Have students say the word, then say each sound as they touch or write it.

A1 Shifty Words	**B1** Rhyming Words
k <u>i</u> t e	s <u>a</u> l e
<u>l</u> i k e	t <u>a</u> l e
l i <u>n</u> e	wh <u>a</u> l e

PROCEDURES

1. First Reading

Mix group and individual turns, independent of your voice. Have students work toward an accuracy goal of 0–2 errors and practice any difficult words.

2. Second Reading, Short Passage Practice: Developing Prosody

- Demonstrate how to read a line or two with expression. Read at a rate slightly faster than the students' rate. Say something like:

  Listen as I read the first two sentences with expression and phrasing. I'm going to emphasize certain words and pause between sentences.

  "Kites have been around a long time, probably more than 2,000 years. Long ago, people used kites when they went fishing."

- Guide practice with your voice. Now read the paragraph with me.

- Provide individual turns while others track with their fingers and whisper read. Provide descriptive and positive feedback.

  [Babak], you read with wonderful expression!

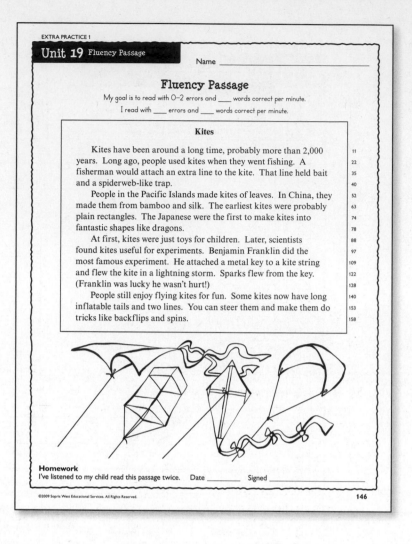

EXTRA PRACTICE 1

Unit 19 Fluency Passage

Name _____

Fluency Passage

My goal is to read with 0–2 errors and ____ words correct per minute.

I read with ____ errors and ____ words correct per minute.

Kites

Kites have been around a long time, probably more than 2,000 years. Long ago, people used kites when they went fishing. A fisherman would attach an extra line to the kite. That line held bait and a spiderweb-like trap. — 11 / 22 / 35 / 40

People in the Pacific Islands made kites of leaves. In China, they made them from bamboo and silk. The earliest kites were probably plain rectangles. The Japanese were the first to make kites into fantastic shapes like dragons. — 52 / 63 / 74 / 78

At first, kites were just toys for children. Later, scientists found kites useful for experiments. Benjamin Franklin did the most famous experiment. He attached a metal key to a kite string and flew the kite in a lightning storm. Sparks flew from the key. (Franklin was lucky he wasn't hurt!) — 88 / 97 / 109 / 122 / 128

People still enjoy flying kites for fun. Some kites now have long inflatable tails and two lines. You can steer them and make them do tricks like backflips and spins. — 140 / 153 / 158

Homework
I've listened to my child read this passage twice. Date _____ Signed _____

146

3. Partner Reading: Repeated Reading (Checkout Opportunity)

While students do Partner Reading, listen to individuals read the passage. Work on accuracy and fluency, as needed.

4. Homework: Repeated Reading

Have students read the story at home.

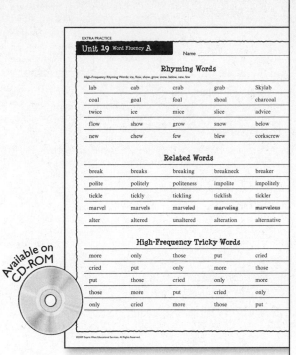

Rhyming Words

High-Frequency Rhyming Words: ice, flow, show, grow, snow, below, new, few

lab	cab	crab	grab	Skylab
coal	goal	foal	shoal	charcoal
twice	ice	mice	slice	advice
flow	show	grow	snow	below
new	chew	few	blew	corkscrew

Related Words

break	breaks	breaking	breakneck	breaker
polite	politely	politeness	impolite	impolitely
tickle	tickly	tickling	ticklish	tickler
marvel	marvels	marveled	**marveling**	**marvelous**
alter	altered	unaltered	alteration	alternative

High-Frequency Tricky Words

more	only	those	put	cried
cried	put	only	more	those
put	those	cried	only	more
those	more	put	cried	only
only	cried	more	those	put

©2009 Sopris West Educational Services. All Rights Reserved.

Available on CD-ROM

EXTRA PRACTICE 1

Unit 19 Activity   Name _____

Passage Comprehension
Kites

Have students read each sentence or question, then fill in the bubble and/or blank with the correct answer. Think aloud with students and discuss possible answers, as needed. Remind students to start with a capital and put a period at the end of each sentence.

1 Long ago, people used kites when they went fishing. A fisherman would attach an extra line that held _bait and a trap._

● bait and a trap   ○ an inflatable tail

2 List three things about how early kites were made.

• People in the Pacific Islands _made kites of leaves._

_____

• People in China _made kites from bamboo and silk._

_____

• People in Japan _were the first to make kites into fantastic_

shapes like dragons.

3 Why did scientists find kites useful? Start with "Scientists found kites useful . . ."

Scientists found kites useful for experiments.

_____

4 What did Benjamin Franklin do that made him famous? Start with "Benjamin Franklin . . ."

Benjamin Franklin attached a metal key to a kite and flew

the kite in a lightning storm.

_____

✓ Check and Correct

©2009 Sopris West Educational Services. All Rights Reserved.   147

PROCEDURES

For each step, demonstrate and guide practice, as needed. Then have students complete the page independently.

1. Activity
Passage Comprehension

• Have students read each sentence or question, then fill in the bubble and/or blank with the correct answer.

• Think aloud with students and discuss the multiple-choice options, as needed.

Self-monitoring

Have students read and check their work, then draw a happy face in the Check and Correct circle.

2. Word Fluency (BLMs are located on the CD.)

• To build fluency, have students read Rhyming Words, Related Words, and High-Frequency Tricky Words. Have students read each section three times in a row.

• To build accuracy, have students read all sets with partners.

ACCURACY BEFORE FLUENCY (Reminder)

Word Fluency is designed to build accuracy and fluency. Students should practice for accuracy before working on fluency.

PROCEDURES

1. Sound Review
Use selected Sound Cards from Units 1–19.

2. Sounding Out Smoothly
- For each word, have students say the underlined part, sound out the word smoothly, then read the whole word. Use the words in sentences, as needed.
- Have students read all the words in the row, building accuracy first, then fluency.
- Repeat practice. Mix group and individual turns, independent of your voice.

3. Accuracy and Fluency Building
- For each task, have students say any underlined part, then read each word.
- Set a pace. Then have students read the whole words in each task and column.
- Provide repeated practice, building accuracy first, then fluency.

4. Tricky Words
Have students read each row for accuracy, then fluency.

5. Multisyllabic Words
For each word, have students read each syllable out loud, then tell how many syllables are in the word. If needed, use the word in a sentence. Have students read the whole word.

6. Dictation

frame, same, sale, came, cave, gave
- Say "frame." Have students say the word. Guide students as they finger count and say the sounds. Have students touch or write the sounds, then read the word.

The first word is *frame.* Say the word. (frame)

What's the first sound? (/fff/) Touch under /fff/.
What's the next sound? (/rrr/) Touch under /rrr/.
What's the next sound? (/āāā/) Write /āāā/.
What's the last sound? (/mmm/) Touch under /mmm/.
Yes, the Bossy E at the end makes letter i say its name.
Read the word. (frame)

- Repeat with "same" and "sale."
- Continue with the shifty words: came, cave, gave.

Unit 19 Decoding Practice

Name _____

1. SOUND REVIEW Use selected Sound Cards from Units 1–19.

2. SOUNDING OUT SMOOTHLY Have students say the underlined part, sound out and read each word, then read the row.

beach	please	crash	couch

3. ACCURACY/FLUENCY BUILDING Have students say any underlined part, then read each word. Next, have students read the column.

A1 Mixed Practice	**B1** Word Endings	**C1** Rhyming Words	**D1** Buildups
weather	sled	pale	board
heavy	sledding	sale	snowboard
after		scale	snowboarding
summer	explore	**C2** Bossy E	**D2** Compound Words
winter	exploring	decided	seashells
desert	cactuses	amazing	snowman
letters	sunny	waves	grandparents
tables	cleaned	state	everything
really	traveled	miles	
	visited		

4. TRICKY WORDS Have students read each row for accuracy, then fluency.

A	above	money	southern	loved	clothes	5
B	built	hours	beautiful	covered	mountains	10

5. MULTISYLLABIC WORDS Have students read the word by parts, tell how many syllables are in the word, then read the whole word.

A	bul·le·tin	bulletin	De·cem·ber	December
B	va·ca·tion	vacation	for·ma·tion	formation
C	mar·vel·ous	marvelous	Cal·i·for·nia	California

6. DICTATION Say the word. Have students say the word, then say each sound as they touch or write it.

A1 Shifty Words	**B1** Shifty Words
frame	came
same	cave
sale	gave

PROCEDURES

1. First Reading

Mix group and individual turns, independent of your voice. Have students work toward an accuracy goal of 0–2 errors and practice any difficult words.

2. Second Reading, Timed Reading: Repeated Reading

- Once the group accuracy goal has been achieved, time individual students for 30 or 60 seconds while the other children track with their fingers and whisper read.

- Determine words correct per minute. Record student scores. Celebrate when students reach their goals!

Wow! [Jordan], you met your goal. That was your best score ever. You get to read to the principal this week.

3. Partner Reading: Repeated Reading (Checkout Opportunity)

While students do Partner Reading, listen to individuals read the passage.

Work on accuracy and fluency, as needed.

4. Homework: Repeated Reading

Have students read the story at home.

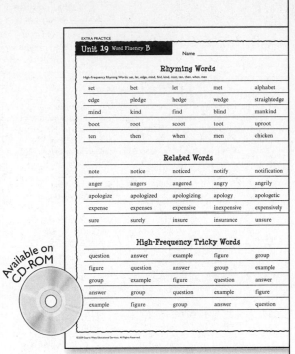

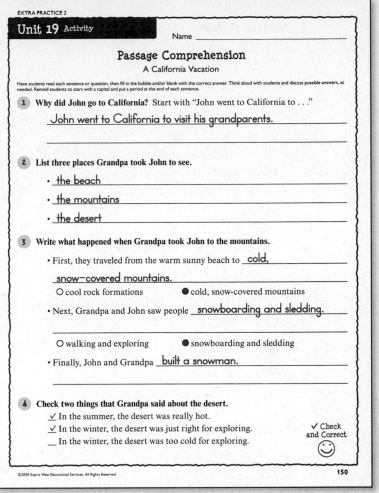

Unit 19 Word Fluency B

Name _____

Rhyming Words

High-Frequency Rhyming Words: set, let, edge, mind, find, kind, root, ten, then, when, men

set	bet	let	met	alphabet
edge	pledge	hedge	wedge	straightedge
mind	kind	find	blind	mankind
boot	root	scoot	toot	uproot
ten	then	when	men	chicken

Related Words

note	notice	noticed	notify	notification
anger	angers	angered	angry	angrily
apologize	apologized	apologizing	apology	apologetic
expense	expenses	expensive	inexpensive	expensively
sure	surely	insure	insurance	unsure

High-Frequency Tricky Words

question	answer	example	figure	group
figure	question	answer	group	example
group	example	figure	question	answer
answer	group	question	example	figure
example	figure	group	answer	question

Available on CD-ROM

Unit 19 Activity

Name _____

Passage Comprehension
A California Vacation

Have students read each sentence or question, then fill in the bubble and/or blank with the correct answer. Think aloud with students and discuss possible answers, as needed. Remind students to start with a capital and put a period at the end of each sentence.

1 **Why did John go to California?** Start with "John went to California to . . ."

John went to California to visit his grandparents.

_____

2 **List three places Grandpa took John to see.**

• the beach

• the mountains

• the desert

3 **Write what happened when Grandpa took John to the mountains.**

• First, they traveled from the warm sunny beach to cold, snow-covered mountains.

○ cool rock formations ● cold, snow-covered mountains

• Next, Grandpa and John saw people snowboarding and sledding.

○ walking and exploring ● snowboarding and sledding

• Finally, John and Grandpa built a snowman.

_____

4 **Check two things that Grandpa said about the desert.**

✓ In the summer, the desert was really hot.

✓ In the winter, the desert was just right for exploring.

___ In the winter, the desert was too cold for exploring.

✓ Check and Correct

☺

150

PROCEDURES

For each step, demonstrate and guide practice, as needed. Then have students complete the page independently.

1. Activity
Passage Comprehension

• Have students read each sentence or question, then fill in the bubble and/or blank, or check the blank with the correct answer.

• Think aloud with students and discuss the multiple-choice options, as needed.

Self-monitoring

Have students read and check their work, then draw a happy face in the Check and Correct circle.

2. Word Fluency (BLMs are located on the CD.)

• To build fluency, have students read Rhyming Words, Related Words, and High-Frequency Tricky Words. Have students read each section three times in a row.

• To build accuracy, have students read all sets with partners.

> **ACCURACY BEFORE FLUENCY (Reminder)**
>
> Word Fluency is designed to build accuracy and fluency. Students should practice for accuracy before working on fluency.

PROCEDURES

1. Sound Review
Use selected Sound Cards from Units 1–19.

2. Sounding Out Smoothly
- For each word, have students say the underlined part, sound out the word smoothly, then read the whole word. (Use the words in sentences, as needed.)
- Have students read all the words in the row, building accuracy first, then fluency.
- Repeat practice. Mix group and individual turns, independent of your voice.

3. Accuracy and Fluency Building
- For each task, have students say any underlined part, then read each word.
- Set a pace. Then have students read the whole words in each task and column.
- Provide repeated practice, building accuracy first, then fluency.

4. Tricky Words
Have students read each row for accuracy, then fluency.

5. Multisyllabic Words
For each word, have students read each syllable out loud, then tell how many syllables are in the word. If needed, use the word in a sentence. Have students read the whole word.

6. Dictation

trade, made, make, thank, bank, blank

- Say "trade." Have students say the word. Guide students as they finger count and say the sounds. Have students touch or write the sounds, then read the word. Say something like:

   The first word is **trade.** Say the word. (trade)

   What's the first sound? (/t/) Touch under /t/.

   What's the next sound? (/rrr/) Touch under /rrr/.

   What's the next sound? (/āāā/) Write /āāā/.

   What's the last sound? (/d/) Touch under /d/.

   Read the word. (trade)

   Yes, the Bossy E at the end makes the letter a say its name.

- Repeat with "made" and "make."
- Continue with the rhyming words: thank, bank, blank.

> **CAUTION**
> Your children may not need Extra Practice. Use assessment results to determine if Extra Practice is needed.

EXTRA PRACTICE 3

Unit 19 Decoding Practice

Name _____

1. SOUND REVIEW Use selected Sound Cards from Units 1–19.

2. SOUNDING OUT SMOOTHLY Have students say the underlined part, sound out and read each word, then read the row.

| m<u>u</u>ch | h<u>a</u>ng | trip | s<u>e</u>ll |

3. ACCURACY/FLUENCY BUILDING Have students say any underlined part, then read each word. Next, have students read the column.

A1 Mixed Practice	**B1** Compound Words	**C1** Word Endings	**D1** Mixed Practice
p<u>ar</u>t	everything	g<u>oes</u>	p<u>er</u>haps
f<u>ir</u>st	everyone	g<u>o</u>ing	p<u>er</u>son
s<u>oo</u>n	anyone	d<u>oi</u>ng	ok<u>ay</u>
b<u>oy</u>s			<u>ag</u>reed
h<u>ea</u>d	**B2** Contractions	**C2** Names and Abbreviations	pl<u>ace</u>s
r<u>oo</u>m	It's	Brandon	r<u>ea</u>lly
f<u>ou</u>nd	I'm	Robert	party
swit<u>ch</u>	I'll	Cara	h<u>or</u>se's
<u>ch</u>ange	We'll	Wilson	<u>s</u>uspect
	Let's	Mrs.	

4. TRICKY WORDS Have students read each row for accuracy, then fluency.

| Ⓐ | idea | wear | brothers | wanted | who | 5 |
| Ⓑ | gone | we're | great | people | earn | 10 |

5. MULTISYLLABIC WORDS Have students read the word by parts, tell how many syllables are in the word, then read the whole word.

Ⓐ	sup•posed	supposed	po•lite	polite
Ⓑ	de•cide	decide	dis•guise	disguise
Ⓒ	civ•i•lized	civilized	re•cog•nize	recognize

6. DICTATION Say the word. Have students say the word, then say each sound as they touch or write it.

A1 Shifty Words	**B1** Rhyming Words
t r <u>a</u> d e	th <u>a</u> n k
<u>m</u> <u>a</u> d e	b <u>a</u> n k
m a <u>k</u> e	bl <u>a</u> n k

151

PROCEDURES

1. First Reading

Mix group and individual turns, independent of your voice. Have students work toward an accuracy goal of 0–2 errors and practice any difficult words.

2. Second Reading, Short Passage Practice: Developing Prosody

- Demonstrate how to read a line or two with expression. Read at a rate slightly faster than the students' rate. Say something like: **Listen as I read the first two sentences with expression and phrasing. I'm going to emphasize certain words and pause between sentences.**

  "Betsy and Cara were going to a party, and everyone was supposed to wear a disguise. The girls were trying to decide what to wear."

- Guide practice with your voice. **Now read the paragraph with me.**

- Provide individual turns while others track with their fingers and whisper read. Provide descriptive and positive feedback. **[Jesika], you read with wonderful expression!**

3. Partner Reading: Repeated Reading (Checkout Opportunity)

While students do Partner Reading, listen to individuals read the passage. Work on accuracy and fluency, as needed.

4. Homework: Repeated Reading

Have students read the story at home.

PROCEDURES

For each step, demonstrate and guide practice, as needed. Then have students complete the page independently.

1. Activity
Passage Comprehension

- Have students read each sentence or question, then fill in the bubble and/or blank with the correct answer.
- Think aloud with students and discuss the multiple-choice options, as needed.

Self-monitoring

Have students read and check their work, then draw a happy face in the Check and Correct circle.

2. Word Fluency (BLMs are located on the CD.)

You may wish to have students repeat practice with Extra Practice, Word Fluency A or B.

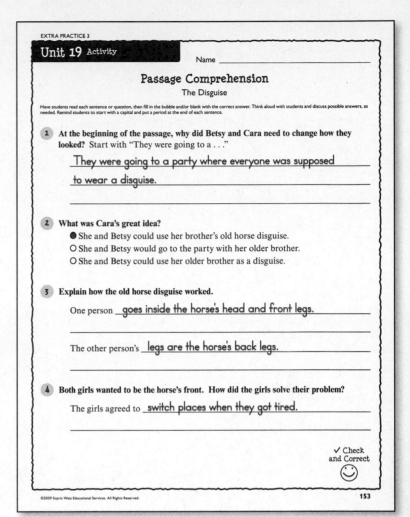

EXTRA PRACTICE 3

Unit 19 Activity

Name _____

Passage Comprehension
The Disguise

Have students read each sentence or question, then fill in the bubble and/or blank with the correct answer. Think aloud with students and discuss possible answers, as needed. Remind students to start with a capital and put a period at the end of each sentence.

1. At the beginning of the passage, why did Betsy and Cara need to change how they looked? Start with "They were going to a . . ."

    They were going to a party where everyone was supposed to wear a disguise.

2. What was Cara's great idea?
    - ● She and Betsy could use her brother's old horse disguise.
    - ○ She and Betsy would go to the party with her older brother.
    - ○ She and Betsy could use her older brother as a disguise.

3. Explain how the old horse disguise worked.

    One person goes inside the horse's head and front legs.

    The other person's legs are the horse's back legs.

4. Both girls wanted to be the horse's front. How did the girls solve their problem?

    The girls agreed to switch places when they got tired.

    ✓ Check and Correct
    ☺

©2009 Sopris West Educational Services. All Rights Reserved.

153

129